O9-BTJ-509

WALKING WITH SPRING

*the first thru-hike
of the Appalachian Trail*

by Earl V. Shaffer

Appalachian Trail Conference
Harpers Ferry, West Virginia

The author and publisher wish to acknowledge the work of the late Florence Nichol of Arlington, Virginia, an Appalachian Trail volunteer for more than four decades, for her valuable editorial assistance in the early 1980s in preparing this manuscript for publication.

Photographs with the text are from slides taken by the author during his historic trek in 1948.

With the exception of the cover, this is a facsimile reprint of the 1983 edition.

Cover background photograph is by Ken Wadness.

ISBN 0-917953-84-3

Library of Congress Catalogue Card Number: 83-71404
Published by the Appalachian Trail Conference
P.O. Box 807, Harpers Ferry, West Virginia 25425

© 2004 Earl Shaffer Foundation. All rights reserved.
No part of this publication may be reproduced or transmitted in any form
or by any means without permission in writing from the publisher.
First printed, privately, in 1981 by the author (1919-2002).
First Appalachian Trail Conference printing, 1983.
Fourth printing, 2004.

Printed and bound in the United Sates of America.

All proceeds from the sale of this book support the management of the Appalachian Trail.

To Benton MacKaye, the Dreamer,
and to the Trail People who
made the Dream come true.

Foreword

It was late at night and a dozen or so hikers were clustered around a man who was picking a guitar and singing. The guitar was old, well used and loved. The man was of no more than medium height, but solidly built, with the kind of rugged face that in about its fortieth year stops aging. The voice, neither elegant nor sophisticated, had a haunting, almost eerie quality that compelled attention. The song spoke of a lonely hiker sitting at Hawk Rock, high above the Susquehanna River, watching below him the lights of Duncannon.

This is one of my earliest recollections of Earl Shaffer. It was at one of the periodic hikers' gatherings that I had started attending; I no longer remember which one, although it doesn't really matter. Earl had drifted in earlier in the day—in a way that I later learned was typical—unannounced and unexpected. His appearance among a group of fellow hikers is perhaps best described as unprepossessing, and it is unlikely that I would have taken any note of this anonymous man had it not been for the knot of people that quickly formed around him. Curious, I edged over to see what was causing the interest, and shortly found myself introduced to Earl Shaffer.

Although I was then relatively new at the hiking game, I had already heard that name many times from many people—spoken sometimes with awe, sometimes with admiration, but always with respect. I was in the presence, I had sense enough to realize, of a man who had made some history.

We exchanged only a few words on that occasion, and Earl spoke with that way he has of looking into the distance while he talks to you, as though he is just waiting for an opportunity to break away and head off by himself to the mountains. I thought at the time that he was merely being polite and was eager to finish our conversation; later I learned that it was his style. Of course, he really does want to be back in the mountains, but that is because he is Earl Shaffer.

Earl is a loner, a poet and a singer; he is also part of the song. He comes and goes like a melody on the wind—drifting from mountain to mountain, and pausing only occasionally (like the first time I met him) to tell his stories and sing his songs for a few who stop to listen. It has taken almost 35 years since his historic hike to bring Earl's big story to commercial publication. But now it will always be with us, even when the author is off wandering the hills.

In words and a style that spring from the mountains themselves, this book speaks to the heart of every hiker who has ever followed a trail. The words are of the earth, but the message is for the spirit. It harks back to the ancient racial memory of the trails of our ancestors: the trails that lead to food, the trails that take us to adventure, the trails that bring us home.

Not long ago Earl was describing to me a tract of land that had been for sale—"on the sunny side of the mountain," as he put it. He had been thinking of buying it as a place to settle down. The deal fell through, however, and some wealthy big city man now has a new summer home in the mountains. Earl seemed a little disappointed at the time, but I think perhaps things worked out for the best. Some people are destined to be wanderers. Earl Shaffer is one of those.

Just stop occasionally, ridgerunner, and let us hear your stories and your songs.

MAURICE J. FORRESTER, JR.

Duboistown, Pennsylvania
February 1983

Contents

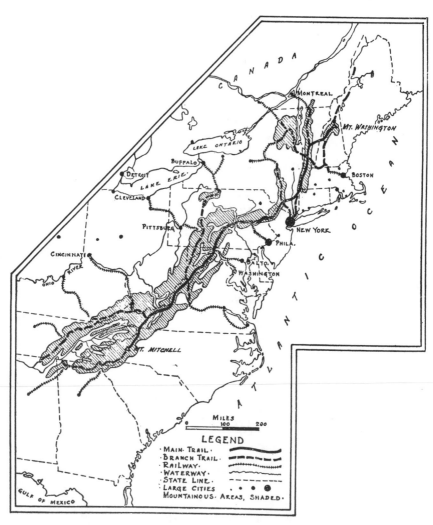

Benton MacKaye's original article proposing the creation of an Appalachian Trail included this map which showed the main Trail extending from Mt. Washington in the north to Mt. Mitchell in the south. Branch trails would reach out in a variety of directions and the entire footpath would be accessible to an area which comprises more than half the population of the U.S. and over one third the population of Canada.

Introduction

TRAIL CALLED APPALACHIAN

THE APPALACHIAN TRAIL, in 1948, had reached a critical point in its history. Maintenance had lapsed in many areas during World War II, with many active workers serving in the armed services. Storm damage, logging operations, and natural growth had erased or cluttered much of the trailway. Marking often was faded or gone. The famous footpath seemed on the way to oblivion.

Even the people who had done most to bring the Trail to tentative completion a few years before the war were doubtful about its future. With this in mind a meeting of the Appalachian Trail Conference was set for June of that year at Fontana Village in North Carolina, to rally the member groups and individuals for an attempt at restoration. While in session the Conference received by mail a message informing them that I had started from Mt. Oglethorpe in Georgia April 4, was now passing through eastern New York State, and was expecting to reach Katahdin in Maine about August 1. The arrival actually was August 5, a total of four months and four hours to cover the 2050-mile trek. So far as is known, this was the first end-to-end continuous trip over the A.T. Publicity by way of an Associated Press story from Millinocket, Maine, written by Mrs. Dean Chase, appeared in many newspapers across the country, and even inspired a few editorials. This, along with stories about the Trail in *National Geographic* and *Readers Digest* and mention in numerous books and magazines, helped revive interest in the Trail project.

Conference officials were skeptical at first. An article had appeared in *Appalachian Trailway News*, written by editor Jean Stephenson and Conference Chairman Myron Avery, while I was en route, explaining why such a trip was almost impossible. Jean was the first Conference official to discuss the trip with me. The discussion was long, held at the dedication of a Potomac Appalachian Trail Club shelter cabin, and actually was a charming but thorough cross examination. Jean, who had a doctorate in law, worked in the Bureau of Supplies and Accounts in the Navy Department. She had a personal library of thousands of books, was a top-ranking genealogist, a conversationalist on any subject, and one of the most dedicated people who ever worked on the Trail project. She said that the first thing Myron Avery said after the newspaper story was, "I wonder if he did." After I submitted a day-by-day report, showed hundreds of color slides, and talked for hours about various parts of the A.T., the trip was accepted as fact. Meanwhile messages came to headquarters from many people who had seen me en route.

Building of the Appalachian Trail had begun twenty-five years before, after publication of an article in the *Journal of the American Institute of Architects* titled "An Appalachian Trail, A Project in Regional Planning." The author was Benton MacKaye, a man of vision whose life was almost a century long. During those busy years he had pioneered some of the basic concepts that have since become vital parts of our way of life. They include the Interstate Highway System, the Tennessee Valley Authority, regional planning of city parks, regional flood control, and rural electrification. He participated with Gifford Pinchot in establishment of national forests and parks. He also was co-founder of The Wilderness Society, co-author of the *Encyclopedia Britannica* article on regional planning, and author of various works on conservation and geotechnics. The Appalachian Trail was his great far-reaching dream and the one for which he is most widely known.

Enthusiasm for the outdoors began for Benton MacKaye when he worked and played as a boy on the farm of Melvin Longley, a highly respected leader in the community of Shirley Center in Massachussetts, who later served in the legislature. Impressions of this formative period in his life and of Mr. Longley were recorded by Mr. MacKaye in an article in the *Finchburg Sentinel* entitled, "A Mountain and a Man." The mountain was Monadnock, a few miles from Shirley Center and across the state line in New Hampshire. This massive pinnacle, jutting far above timberline, was the first high mountain he ever saw and climbed. It gives a panoramic view of the Appalachian Mountain Chain through Connecticut, Massachusetts, Vermont, and New Hampshire, and even shows the tip of Katahdin in Maine on a clear day. It is the only point from which all of the New England states, including Rhode Island, can be seen. Directly north are the massive peaks of the White Mountains, where an extensive trail system already was maintained by the Appalachian Mountain Club. This organization was the first of its kind in America and for many years was the largest. During his college years Mr. MacKaye met and hiked with members of the club.

Benton MacKaye graduated from Harvard in 1900. The following summer he and a friend hiked the length of the Green Mountains in Vermont, following existing paths and woods roads when possible and crossing all major summits. This approximate route was opened up later as the Long Trail by the Green Mountain Club. One of the summits is Stratton Mountain.

One day while gazing from a treetop on Stratton Mountain he had a sudden realization of the almost endless reaches of the Appalachian Chain from Maine to Georgia and the potential for a trail along its crest. It could be patterned after the Long Trail but be at

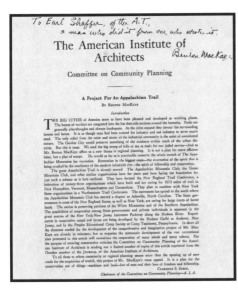

The idea of an Appalachian Trail was first outlined in a 1921 article by forester and philosopher Benton MacKaye. When MacKaye met the first man to hike the entire Trail in one continuous trip, he presented a copy of his article, inscribed to "a man who did it from one who wrote it."

least ten times as long. He spoke of this to various friends over a period of perhaps ten years before Clarence Stein, an editor of the *Journal of the American Institute of Architects,* finally declared, "Ben, I am tired of hearing you talk about this and doing nothing. You write it and I'll publish it." The result was the article appearing in October of 1921. A printers copy of that article inscribed, "To one who did it from one who wrote it" was given to me thirty years later in his home at Shirley Center by Benton MacKaye.

The article, with an introduction by Mr. Stein, described the Trail over the full length of the Appalachian skyline, with the northern anchor to be Mt. Washington in New Hampshire and the southern anchor to be Mt. Mitchell in North Carolina. He saw it as a master trail for a network of side trails to points of interest or outdoor-oriented activity. Open shelters would be provided at intervals. The work would be done by volunteers and suitable organizations would be set up along the trailway to facilitate activities. The accompanying sketch map showed the approximate route, with branch trails extending beyond. Routing the Trail over Mt. Mitchell later was abandoned in favor of the Smokies, and extensions into Maine and Georgia were included as part of the master trail.

Ten years later Mr. MacKaye wrote an article appearing in the April 1932 *Scientific Monthly,* in which he assessed the progress of the project, the forming of the Appalachian Trail Conference in 1925 as a confederation of local clubs, the completion of about two-thirds of the trailway, and a general summary of the regions traversed.

During my first visit with Benton MacKaye at his home in Shirley Center several years after "The Long Cruise," he spoke of the early days of the Trail project, when he talked with anyone who would listen at points along the Trail route. One of these meetings was with the Blue Mountain Eagle Climbing Club of Reading, Pennsylvania, which had been organized several years earlier. One of the members was Daniel Hoch. "Danny," as he was affectionately known to his many friends, later was elected to the U.S. House of Representatives from Berks County. While serving in Washington in 1945 he introduced a bill providing for Federal protection of the A.T. as part of a national system of foot trails. This protection was imperative because about half the trailway passed over private lands, where it was in constant jeopardy. Unfortunately, this legislation, though re-introduced periodically, was not passed by Congress until 1968. By that time much of the wilderness aspect of the Appalachian Crest had vanished forever.

The first sections of the Appalachian Trail were borrowed from the Long Trail and the Appalachian Mountain Club Trail System. The first few miles built especially for the project were in Palisades Interstate Park, with Benton MacKaye participating. Leaders in this were Raymond H. Torrey of the Palisades Interstate Park Trail Conference, which had been organized two years before, and Major W.A. Welch, manager and engineer for the park. Major Welch also designed the A.T. symbol that has long been the signature of the Trail. The Palisades organization later was expanded into the New York-New Jersey Trail Conference. Progress was made elsewhere the next few years and new clubs were formed. One of these, in Washington, was the Potomac Appalachian Trail Club.

In 1926 Arthur Perkins, a retired lawyer from Connecticut, took over active leadership of the project and worked tirelessly until his death in 1930. He is credited by Myron Avery, his successor, with developing the momentum that assured completion of the project. Actually, Captain Avery contributed as much or more and continued as chairman of the Appalachian Trail Conference until his death in 1952. He was a very determined and dedicated man who worked ceaselessly in locating, building, and measuring the Trail, spending hours in the headquarters at night, in addition to his full-time job as an admiralty lawyer in the Judge Advocate General's Office of the Navy. He was the first person to traverse all of the Trail route over a period of years, and pushed his measuring wheel over every bit of it at least once. One of the Bigelow peaks in his native state of Maine has since been re-named for him.

Another important contribution of Captain Avery is his detailed history of the Trail's early development. He told of the individuals who pioneered the route in remote areas, the most outstanding feat being, in his opinion, the opening of the Barren-Chairback Range by Walter D. Greene, Broadway actor and Maine guide. This dramatic effort through "a wilderness of spruce and fir quite beyond the scope of amateur effort," along with the labors of Captain Avery and other individuals and groups, resulted finally in completion of the rugged Maine section. The last link of the entire Maine-to-Georgia route was built on the south side of Sugarloaf Mountain, second highest peak in Maine, in 1937, providing a continuous hiking footpath the length of the Appalachians. The Appalachian Trail Conference was organized in 1925 to coordinate the work of the clubs and individuals who were trying to make the Appalachian Trail a reality. Today it is the private, nationwide organization that represents citizens' interests in the Appalachian Trail. Its affairs are controlled by a Board of Managers, under a Conference Chairman and three Vice-Chairmen who are elected by the members of the Conference. A headquarters for the ATC was furnished in Washington for many years by the Potomac Appalachian Trail Club. In 1972 the headquarters was moved to Harpers Ferry, West Virginia.

Many individuals and groups were and still are involved in trail building and maintenance. Communication is vital. The *Appalachian Trailway News* was pioneered in 1939 by Jean Stephenson and she edited it for many years. She dedicated a large part of her life to Trail work, as did Marion Park, longtime Secretary, and Murray Stevens, who succeeded Myron Avery as Chairman at a critical time. Without such dedicated "Trail People" the project would long since have languished. It is my privilege to have known and worked with some of them. For instance, Murray Stevens, then living in New York City and commuting to staff meetings in Washington, also came to Pennsylvania over several weekends to join me in scouting, marking, and measuring the sixty-mile relocation made necessary by the establishment of the Indiantown Gap Military Reservation.

The years following the Fontana meeting saw a great effort by Trail people to restore and improve the trailway. In this I joined, at Captain Avery's insistence, as Corresponding Secretary of the Conference and meanwhile worked for the establishment of the Susquehanna Appalachian Trail Club at Harrisburg and the Keystone Trails Association. At the same time extensive relocations were underway at Roan Mountain in North Carolina and southwest of Roanoke in Virginia. These relocations totaled hundreds of miles and eliminated many miles of road walking. Many shorter relocations and the building of many shelters, including several by myself, greatly improved the entire picture.

In 1951 Gene Espy, of Georgia, duplicated my south-to-north trip, starting the end of May after college graduation, and completing the trek in snowy conditions. The same year, Chester Dziengielewski of Connecticut and Martin Papendick of Michigan started at Katahdin and reached Oglethorpe in October. This was the beginning of an ever-increasing number of hikers "doing" the A.T.

In 1965 considering that so much of the Trail had been changed, I decided to make a sentimental journey and traverse the Trail in the opposite direction, from north to south. This trek began

July 20 in cold, rainy weather and ended ninety-nine days later during freezing weather at Springer Mountain. The southern terminus had been changed years before because of encroachment on Oglethorpe.

Private ownership of land over which the Trail passes has always been a problem, but since 1968 when the National Trails System Act designated the Appalachian Trail as one of the nation's first National Scenic Trails, federal and state actions have made considerable progress toward achieving permanent protection for the Trail route. Favorable Congressional appropriations for land acquisition in 1978 enabled the National Park Service, along with the U.S. Forest Service, and the states, to increase efforts to provide a permanent route and "buffer zone." The goal is protection of the entire length of the A.T. by 1985.

I suggested several years ago that expansion of the original project was logical. Trails are being built along the Alleghenies, west of the Great Valley, by local groups, much as the A.T. was built. These could be linked together and then joined at the southern and northern ends with the existing trail to form a giant loop about five thousand miles long, a truly endless trail that would encompass the entire Appalachian Mountain System. I am certain that Benton MacKaye would have concurred enthusiastically. He died several years ago at the age of ninety-seven, but his spirit lives on in his writings, in The Wilderness Society, and in the world-famous trail he fathered more than sixty years ago.

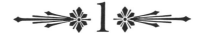

The Cloud-High Hills

*There's a lone footpath along the crest
of the Appalachian Chain,
On the cloud-high hills so richly blest
with sun and wind and rain.*

> OGLETHORPE
> SOUTHERN TERMINUS OF THE
> APPALACHIAN TRAIL, A MOUNTAIN
> FOOTPATH EXTENDING 2050 MILES
> TO MOUNT KATAHDIN IN MAINE

THE BOARD SIGN was battered and weatherbeaten, its posts held up by a heap of gathered stones. A wintry wind gusted across the bleak and isolated summit, rustling brown leaves among the scraggly grass and muttering through the surrounding trees and brush. Midway of the clearing stood a tall white shaft of native marble, honoring the founder of the state of Georgia. Below the sunrise lay the Piedmont foothills deep in shadow. Southward and barely visible in the early daylight was Stone Mountain, near the city of Atlanta. To the west stretched the rolling countryside of northwestern Georgia and the little town of Jasper. I had come to Oglethorpe the previous day by way of the town, after a journey from Gainesville, first on foot and then on a ramshackle and overloaded bus.

In Jasper, when asked which of the peaks on the eastern skyline was Oglethorpe, a man hesitated before drawling, "I don't rightly know, Mister, but it's one of them tops out there." Along a gravel road in that direction, a logging truck stopped and the driver offered a ride. As we rattled along, a boy riding on the back mentioned that another hiker had started the week before, adding, "At least you won't need to worry about rattlesnakes. It's too early for them to be crawlin'." At the ridge crest they directed me along the gravel road leading southward to the peak. Soon a truck came lurching along and the driver asked if I had seen his foxhounds, which had gotten loose and were chasing deer. He gave me his phone number in case I saw them but didn't say where I was to call from.

Reaching the summit of Oglethorpe near sundown and finding it exposed to a cold and merciless wind, I backtracked to a rickety leanto near a rickety firetower and stayed there. The Little Black Notebook says, "Got cold and blustery toward morning, hated like poison to get up." At least the scramble back to the summit warmed me up a little. And now the time had come. This was the threshold of my great adventure, long delayed by World War II and without my trail partner, who had been killed on Iwo Jima. Those four and a half years of army service, more than half of it in combat areas of the Pacific, without furlough or even rest leave, had left me confused and depressed. Perhaps this trip would be the answer.

Late in 1947 I had seen an article in an outdoor magazine entitled "The Long Trail's Challenge." It said that no one was known to have hiked the entire Trail in a continuous journey, though many had tried, and such a trip might actually be impossible. Suddenly the old dream came alive. Why not walk the army out of my system, both mentally and physically, take pictures and notes along the way, make a regular expedition out of it? The Trail would benefit at a time when it was at low ebb. My background of "running the brush" in all kinds of weather, based on the writings of such men as Nessmuk and Gray Owl, should carry me through. Surely those years of trailing with Walter, when we first heard of the Appalachian Trail and wanted to walk it, would be an asset now.

The launching of the "Long Cruise" was totally lacking in ceremony. I looked at the battered sign for the last time while the shrill wind seemed to be saying, "Get moving, Ridgerunner, the Trail is calling and Katahdin is far away." My Mountain Troop rucksack was bulky and heavy as I slung it to my shoulders and started off. In it were an Air Corps survival tent, a Marine Corps poncho, a rainhat, a "paper mill" blanket, Marble Company matchsafe and compass and sheath knife, small handaxe, sewing kit, snake-bite kit, Mountain Troop cook kit, and food for about a week. Clothing consisted of T-shirts, Navy turtleneck, Mountain Cloth pants, wool-cotton socks, and Birdshooter boots. The only item not with me all the way was the tent. It stayed with me about a week.

My plan was to move north with the spring, with the seasonal change, with no definite day-by-day goals but never tarrying long, as weather and terrain permitted. The early start from the south would allow a maximum of at least six months to reach and cross the timberline of New England. I hoped to maintain an average daily distance of close to twenty miles but would settle for fifteen. Another advantage of the early start was the absence of snakes and bugs. Also, in April—true first month of the year—the woods are at their finest, with the budding and leafing of trees, the blooming of flowers, the full flowing streams and waterfalls, the rainswept blue of the sky. And the little old Retina, rugged and dependable, would record the beautiful scenes.

Breakfast was cooked at the rickety leanto, which did provide a fire pit and water from a nearby spring. Next stop was at the road crossing where the loggers had left me the day before. Here I managed a self portrait, with delayed action shutter release, showing a rear view of myself and pack with the lake at Connahaynee Lodge in the background. The pack looks heavy and it was, but not for long. My shoulders already were sore and some adjustments obviously were necessary. Ben Franklin, one of the wisest men who ever lived, once said, "Experience keeps a dear school but fools learn in no other." The lesser fools are those who learn in a hurry. By rearranging the contents of the pack to cause a forward shift in weight and by discarding the large back pocket it was possible to ease the burden. Long distance backpacking is a rugged business and should be handled accordingly. Both bulk and weight are hindrances and must be kept to a minimum. My motto is "Carry as little as possible but choose that little with care."

Meanwhile a few wild flowers were blooming in sheltered spots and sometimes a holly tree would contrast its brilliant red berries and glossy green leaves with the still leafless forest. Wild creatures were plentiful. Once a wild turkey flushed a few feet ahead, squawking and beating its wings, setting me back on my heels. Other times quail, woodcock, or grouse caused similar disturbances. The weather had been sunny but now a buttermilk sky was moving in, foretelling rain. About noon the Trail crossed a road gap, probably the site of Southern's Store, mentioned in early guidebooks, and entered a picnic area near a reservoir. Just then four girls came strolling over a rise ahead. They were identically dressed in snowy blouses and long black "new look" skirts, a very charming foursome. My T-shirt, gray pants, helter-skelter hair, and sweaty face were definitely not as stylish. They passed quite sedately, but one of them muttered what sounded like "huba huba."

Beyond the rise a family of three was setting out a picnic lunch. As I was passing, the man looked up and said casually, "Howdy, where you headin'?" Just as casually I replied, "To Maine." A poke in the solar plexis would have produced the same result. His jaw sagged and his eyes widened. When informed of my trek he admitted he had never heard of the Appalachian Trail. Meanwhile the lady just stood there and stared. Suddenly she spoke, "Y'all mean to say you are walkin' all the way to Maine, over the mountains, all by yourself, and carryin' that thing?" The answer was obvious, "Yes Ma'am." She stared a moment longer, then shook her head and chuckled. "I'm glad I got sense, Mister, I'm glad I got sense." The little boy said absolutely nothing. The man said, "Well, good luck to ye."

A while later the Trail passed Amicalola Falls, one of the highest east of the Rockies, totaling more than five hundred feet of cascades and a sheer drop of more than a hundred feet. The falls can be heard at least a mile away. I tried to crawl down to get a picture but

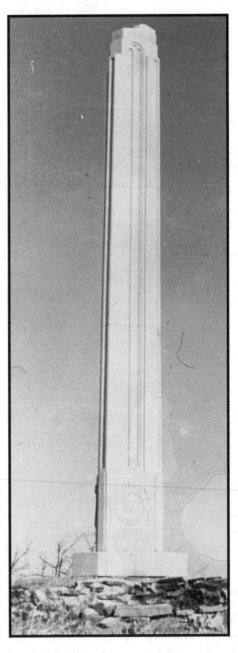

The Oglethorpe Memorial on Mt. Oglethorpe, originally marked the southern end of the A.T. The southern terminus of the A.T. is now on Springer Mountain, to the north and east of Mt. Oglethorpe.

thickets of rhododendron drenched with spray were too discouraging. A state park is located below and the approach is easier there. The Trail from the falls to Springer Mountain is now an approach trail. The Trail south of the falls has been abandoned.

Toward evening the Trail came to Frosty Mountain Tower. So far the way had been clearly marked. Suddenly, it wasn't. I was casting around like a busy hound when the warden on the tower noticed my antics and came out on the catwalk to shout directions. This helped a little, but the next few miles were disrupted by logging, and marking was poor. At twilight the path was upslope over rough and rocky terrain while the sky clouded over. Just before deep dark, when stopping was a must, I spotted a giant fallen chestnut tree held off the ground by limb stubs. I crawled under, wrapped in blanket and poncho, and fell into exhausted sleep, despite small sticks and stones underneath. Alas! No rest for the weary. About midnight a shower of cold rain blew into my sanctuary. With fortitude born of desperation I rolled out and hunted by flashlight for slabs of bark to shield the windward side, then at dawn packed hurriedly and hastened on, telling myself that the lady the day before had been absolutely right.

Rain still fell as the Lone Expedition crossed the summit of Springer Mountain. This is the southernmost point in the great loop of the Blue Ridge, with the eastern arm including Mt. Mitchell and the western arm the Great Smokies, the two joining again in southern Virginia.

This loop encompasses the highest peaks and most massive ridges east of the Mississippi. At the time my only concern was hunger and thirst. On the far slope was a good spring and there I managed to cook the first meal since the previous noon. Cornmeal mush, with raisins and brown sugar and canned milk, tasted mighty good right then. Such food isn't fancy but it sticks.

The rain continued and fog rolled in, dense and muggy in low spots, shifting and swirling farther up, as the Trail came to a wire-enclosed area. Which way did the Trail turn? Trees were moss-spotted. Marking was faded. Because of mail difficulties at home I had not received maps and data ordered from the Appalachian Trail Conference, and now had nothing but a road map to guide me. It showed the A.T. as a vaguely dotted line. I tried the northwesterly side and had gone at least seven miles along the boundary when a traveled road appeared where none should have been. I was sitting on a bank and staring at my road map when a feeling of eyes upon me drew my attention up the road. It was a barefooted mountain boy looking as though he wanted to run, but he came on bravely. Within a minute we were friends. He said he reckoned the Trail went on the other side of the Game Refuge, adding in his winsome drawl that his pappy was off to Ellijay in his car or he would drive me back along the fireroad. I thanked the little feller as he continued homeward, while memories came of my own boyhood among the Rolling Hills.

Cloud-High Hills 11

Getting back to the Trail was wearisome, especially on blistered and aching feet. Trying to favor the blisters resulted in jarring arches, knees, and hip joints to the point where they joined the clamor. Every bump and twist on the rocky fireroad was an added misery. Hiking had become an exquisite kind of torture. Something must be done. Since the weather was too cold and footing too rocky to allow walking barefoot, the regular solution, the next best thing was to put sand in my boots and wear no socks until my feet toughened. This was painful at first but calluses finally formed. Generous use of Quinsana foot powder also helped. Actually, I have learned since that the sand is not necessary; that hiking without socks on a rugged trip is the best way to avoid foot troubles. Naturally I do not expect this to be believed or adopted by others. But the Indian ways are usually best in the woods.

The rain had eased during my wrong-going but resumed as the trek continued from the point of wrong-turning. The fog was worse than ever, so there is no recollection of ascending the "Winding Stairs" or of entering the Chattahoochee National Forest; but I do recall stopping to drink at Rattlesnake Spring. Darkness caught me at Frying Pan Gap, just then a morass of mud and dripping trees. All but one of my matches were used before the fire finally burned. A pot of tea was all I could manage. That night was thoroughly miserable. The tent was poorly designed and almost useless. Finally came the dawn and another "soon start." The rain continued as the Trail alternated from woods roads to brushy timber.

Once a truckload of men, probably a Forest Service crew on flood duty, came by as I was standing under a tree to lessen the brunt of an especially heavy downpour. They stared as though they didn't believe their eyes. At twilight I blundered into Cane Creek Gap and pitched camp. Fortunately, a pitchpine snag furnished fuel that would burn under such conditions and I managed a cooking and drying fire. The Little Black Notebook says that oatmeal, with brown sugar and canned milk, was on the menu.

Meanwhile a thunderstorm was approaching and firewood had to be stockpiled, so I was out there hacking at the pine snag, which isn't easy under a poncho. Wind rose to a wail and thunder crashed and rolled, then lulled for an instant. Suddenly, out of the eerie silence came a screeching wail from close by in the woods. Something cold poured along my spine and my hair rose up like rooster hackles. A few seconds later, back by the fire, I realized it was only a wildcat and not a mountain lion. Those critters seem to delight in such doings. Since a fire won't burn without wood it was necessary to venture out again later. About midnight the sky cleared and stars shone clear as gems on jet black velvet. A cold wind swept the mountain, and I shivered in spite of the fire. Such a night is guaranteed to instill a profound respect for the power of nature and the vastness of the universe. Once in the wee small hours a line from

Kipling went through my mind: "Who has smelled woodsmoke at twilight, who has seen the campfire burning, who is quick to read the noises of the night?"

Soon after starting in the morning, and while considering the need for matches, I heard a hound baying in the valley northward. After listening a bit to make sure it was stationary, I turned in that direction. The sun was shining brightly now and the temperature rising, so I stopped at a small stream to remove the grime accumulated during the previous days. Standing in a spot of sunshine helped lessen the shock of the icy water but it still was drastic treatment. Half an hour later I came to a small farm in a cove. It was a nicer place than usually seen in the back country, the buildings painted and a lawn around the house. A tall young man was digging a trench for a water line from an uphill spring. He listened to my story, gave me what matches he was carrying, then headed for the house to get more. When offered payment he shook his head and smiled. Meanwhile the hound I had heard, and several others, were watching sullenly and growling. He spoke in a low voice to control them. I told of knowing a hound-dog man from Kentucky while in the service who said, "The more you yell at a dog the less it'll mind." The young man nodded and smiled again.

When asked about getting back to the A.T. he directed me to a "road"—about four feet wide—which he said would take me to "the Government Trail." Near the crest of the ridge I spotted a blaze and resumed the trek, hurrying along for several miles then stopping aghast. Before me was my campsite in Cane Creek Gap, clearly proven by traces of my fire. Once again it was necessary to sit down and calm my spinning brain. The explanation was simple. On the way up from the farm I had crossed the overgrown Trail on a switchback, caught it at the wrong place, and headed in the wrong direction. Such shenanigans are strictly un-skookum when trudging two thousand miles.

South of Cane Creek Gap, about eight miles, is the town of Dahlonega, where gold mines operated during the eighteen forties. More than sixteen million dollars worth of gold was mined and a government mint was located there during the heyday. An Indian child had found a yellow pebble in a stream and then some gold washed free when a newly built mill race was opened. The diggings were nearly exhausted when the California gold rush began. The miners prepared to leave and a town official tried to persuade them to stay. He pointed dramatically and declared, "Thar's gold in them thar hills." The miners carried that slogan westward. Ironically, the Spanish explorer De Soto passed through this region three hundred years before, searching for gold. He penetrated deep into the southern Appalachians with an Indian princess as hostage guide. She led him inland, probably as far as the Smokies, before escaping. Most of De Soto's expedition was lost before he managed to reach the coast.

The gold strike at Dahlonega was the decisive event leading to "the Trail of Tears," in which the U.S. Army drove the Cherokee Nation westward to Oklahoma in the dead of winter. Many women and children died during this march. One army man who later was an officer in the Confederate army said the Trail of Tears was worse than anything he saw in the Civil War. Originally the Cherokees occupied the entire region from northern Georgia through the western part of the Carolinas, eastern Tennessee, and southern Virginia. Disease and rum, brought by white settlers, and a series of wars resulting from broken treaties had reduced the Cherokee Nation from at least a half million to about twenty thousand. After discovery of the Dahlonega Lode the state of Georgia declared the remaining lands of the Cherokees to be state owned and demanded back rent. The federal government backed the state by driving the Cherokee Nation west.

Starting again from Cane Creek Gap the Lone Expedition passed through a region of knolls, some sheathed in ice where water oozed from rock ledges. Then a tall peak topped by a firetower loomed ahead, but the Trail circled the mountain and came out to a highway in Woody Gap. After hiding the pack in the woods I headed for Suches, a sprawling community near a reservoir on the west slope. The grocery was small, just recently opened, and the choice was limited. The lady went for sugar from her own supply. Otherwise my purchases were a quarter pound of cheese, a loaf of bread, a box of matches, and some small cans of Vienna sausage. Meanwhile people began to drift in, probably to get a look at the stranger. One was a little old mountain lady wearing an ancient shawl. "You ain't agonna sleep on Old Bloody Mountain tonight, be ye?" she queried. I said I didn't know. "Well I wouldn't no how," she declared. "It's too wild lonesome up thar."

The sun was low as the trek continued from Woody Gap. Logging had removed many trees and marking was scarce. Deer leaped ahead in shadowy silhouette against the sunset. In the deep dusk I stopped by a little stream at the edge of an isolated hill farm. The evening was balmy, a welcome change. Then a whip-poor-will called, the first heard on the trip. Late at night another thundergust roared by and the sky still was stormy in the morning. Breakfast was cooking—cornmeal and raisins—over a tiny fire when the jingle of harness alerted me to a man driving a team of mules across the nearby field, probably on his way to a logging operation. Suddenly he stopped and scanned the trees. He had scented the fire. Such vigilance is instinctive with mountain people. Wildfire is one of their worst enemies. When I called and told him I was trail-hiking, he said he had been wondering how a fire could get started on such a wet day.

Intermittent rain fell as I traveled on. Once I left my rainhat by a spring and had to go back a half mile to retrieve it. Then the path slanted steeply upward to a gap and turned on a brushy incline,

A carpet of bluets filled this section of northern Georgia known as "The Swag of the Blue Ridge."

emerging finally on the rocky summit of Blood Mountain. This unusual peak, sacred to the Cherokees, is the highest point on the A.T. in Georgia at an elevation of 4463 feet. Near the top is a stone cabin, complete with fireplace. According to legend it is the home of the Nunnehi, friendly spirit folk, little people with hair reaching to the ground. This mountain was the site of a great battle in which the Cherokees defeated the Creeks, their traditional foes.

The view from Blood Mountain is extraordinary, with jumbled peaks and ridges in every direction. Shadows from broken clouds were moving in ever-changing shapes across the forested slopes. To the south lay the valley of the Chestatee River toward Dahlonega. To the north lay the headwaters of Nottely River and the reservoir. While watching the moving shadows I noticed they were converging. A thunderhead was forming above the peak. Had the Nunnehi decided they didn't like the intruder? No wonder the little old lady in Suches had spoken the way she did. By the time I was a mile down the trail the summit was hidden in swirling rain. And the storm followed me down to Neels Gap, not letting me side-travel to De Soto or Natla Falls. According to Cherokee myth, Neels Gap is the home of the Great Frog, leader of the ancient animal council. By the side of the highway is Wala-siyi Inn, of massive stone and log construction, maintained for the tourist trade in the state park.

Because of the howling storm I took shelter in the wide patio of the inn, which had not yet opened for the season. As the storm was ending a truck came up the highway and I rushed out to ask the driver to mail some post cards. My folks had warned that they would contact the Rangers if they failed to hear from me for more than five days at a time. The driver lingered to talk, said he had lived all his life in that area but hadn't known about the Appalachian Trail. A marker across the road from the inn recounted some of the Cherokee myths of the region. Another marker, placed there by the Georgia Appalachian Trail Club, showed a hiker with a pack stepping forth and the inscription "Appalachian Trail, Georgia to Maine." This was the only place along the entire Trail where the south-to-north designation was seen. Why not designate all the southern half the same way?

From Neels Gap the Trail crossed Levelland Mountain, with the weather turning very cold as I reached a spring at twilight. The temperature dropped so low that my fingers were numb when fetching water in the morning. Then a fine shelter materialized at Tesnatee Gap, no more than a mile away. That storm at Blood Mountain had really knocked things out of shape. Once again I thought of the little old lady at Suches and her talk of "Old Bloody Mountain." Years later I stayed in the stone cabin overnight and wouldn't you know—a howling thundergust.

Beyond Tesnatee Gap the Trail turned north. Within this curve of the Blue Ridge are the uppermost springs and streams of the watershed that supplies Nottely Reservoir. These waters, incredibly, flow northwestwardly through mountain country all the way to the Tennessee River, which flows westward to the Mississippi, which in turn flows south to the Gulf of Mexico. The Trail route crossed overgrown fields and open summits such as Strawberry Top and Sheep Rock Mountain to Horsetrough Mountain, elevation 4057, with a fine view westward of valley farmlands. Early flowers such as bluets were blooming on the high meadows. Sometimes squirrels ran headlong on the ground or scrambled through the treetops. Near Chattahoochee Gap a high ridge forks northward to Brasstown, or Enota Bald, elevation 4768. This is the highest peak in Georgia and can be reached by five miles of side trail.

Soon the Trail swung eastward, still along the water divide. To the south, within this curve, are the headwaters of the Chattahoochee River, extolled by the poet Sidney Lanier. The northernmost springs are at trailside. Instead of flowing to the Atlantic Ocean the Chattahoochee swings south and westward to the Gulf of

Mexico at a point less than three hundred miles from the Mississippi Delta, where the flow from Nottely Watershed finally reaches tidewater. Rocky Knob Shelter loomed by midafternoon, too early to stop. Its roof was caved in anyway. A sign nearby said Montray Shelter was eight and a half miles distant. Those miles seemed mighty long. Perhaps they had been measured in nautical miles by that famous measuring wheel. More likely it was because they were the last of twenty-five. The plodding was interrupted once at Unicoi Gap, where a sign said this was the first road over the Georgia Blue Ridge, built by pioneers and a party of Cherokees. Just then a rattletrap car came chugging by and half a dozen youngsters hung out the windows to stare.

At twilight I came to Tray Mountain Campground. This was the site of "The Old Cheese Factory," one of several established before 1900 in the southern mountains as part of a plan to provide "local industries." No trace of it remains. Thinking the shelter might be on the summit as at Blood Mountain, I kept on but soon I knew I wouldn't make it. My knees wobbled and my head whirled. Sitting down was the only way to avoid falling. By sheer will power I unpacked everything that could be wrapped around me for warmth and stretched out on the Trail. After strength returned I reached the top and found only a tripod of poles. Returning dejectedly to the campground, I hunted wood by flashlight, cooked supper, and finally bedded down about midnight. Never again on the Long Cruise would I come so near to total collapse. Next day the shelter proved to be only a half mile beyond the summit.

Montray Shelter would have been useless anyway because cattle had broken down the fence and used it like a stable. A nearby sign said Snake Mountain Shelter was ten miles away. The first few were over "The Swag of the Blue Ridge," a long open area where cattle, hogs, and horses were grazing. Bells sounded occasionally and almost any kind of livestock might be encountered. Hundreds of hogs were rooting for sprouted acorns. Once a gigantic sow with at least a dozen in her litter got so pugnacious it was necessary to circle past. Next came Dismal Mountain and Dismal Gap, but the weather was very pleasant and ground flowers and dogwood were blooming. Sometimes a vista would open eastward to Burton Reservoir. On Kelly Knob two grouse flushed underfoot and then a whitetail deer went leaping away. Snake Mountain Cabin was reached by midafternoon and proved to be the best shelter yet, with a good spring and a fireplace inside, a good place to pause and regroup.

Someone had used the cabin as a winter camp for horseback travel. Below the spring was a pole corral. Inside was a pile of hay that would soften my bed. Out front in the mud were footprints, probably of the man who had started on Easter Sunday. He couldn't be more than two days ahead or rain would have blotted the tracks. My map indicated a nearby woods road would lead to a small town in the valley westward and my supplies were low, so I left my gear in the shelter and ventured forth. Within a mile I regretted it. This was a well-watered region of dense laurel thickets, ideal for the making of "Mountain Dew." A certain odor soon was evident and you can be sure I didn't linger or look to right or left. When I passed through the village farther down someone was outside at every place but no one seemed to notice me; this gave me a very nervous feeling.

Beyond the village was a ramshackle store. The keeper was nearly blind, which meant finding the stuff myself and even reading the price tags. For obvious reasons I decided to return to the ridge crest by the public road. About halfway a young mountain man stopped to offer a lift. He had been in the navy in the Pacific so we soon were practically buddies. He asked point blank if I wasn't afraid to walk the mountains alone in strange country, even on the "Government Trail." He seemed to be genuinely concerned; said he had made "licker" himself for almost two years until he and his partner were almost caught one night. He pointed to a roadside bank where they had jettisoned the contraband that time, then to the ravine— where I had just descended—and remarked that four stills had been raided there the week before. No wonder I had smelled something, and no wonder the villagers had been hostile.

When Snake Mountain Cabin was mentioned he said he knew the place, in fact had penned his hogs there sometimes when rounding them up. The pesky things were wild and had to be caught one by one. When we reached the Trail crossing he wanted me to go along to Clayton for a "high old time." My excuse was approaching sunset and my gear at the shelter. Rain began falling as I arrived and continued through the night. For once I was dry and warm. The morning weather was atrocious, clammy cold with heavy mist sifting through and clinging to the trees. Footing was muddy and marking faint. Heavy fog rolled. The Trail slanted upward beyond the road gap and came to a rock ledge at the North Carolina state line. Pausing there to rest I looked back over the first week. It had been a feverish struggle over rugged terrain in rainy weather. My average daily distance was about fifteen miles, the minimum calculated for going all the way.

2

Land of the Noonday Sun

Far bells were somewhere ringing,
Out on the mountains high,
Their silver voices singing
Allegro to the sky.

THE FOG WAS BURNING OFF as the Lone Expedition crossed into North Carolina. The forest growth showed fresh and green as brilliant sunlight broke through. Then horse tracks appeared along an uphill stretch for at least a mile. Thinking the rider might be a beautiful southern belle on a morning meander I even went to the trouble of combing my hair. The tracks finally turned aside, suggesting that a cattleman was checking livestock, chiefly hogs. Whenever I neared a group they would scatter pellmell while bells on the leaders would tinkle merrily. Foraging is allowed on National Forest lands of the south, just as in the western states.

Nantahala is a Cherokee name meaning "Land of the Noonday Sun," a fitting name for a region where ravines are so deep and the slopes so steep that lowlands are in shadow most of the time. Often the slopes are so heavily covered with brush and greenbrier that the tops of the spurs and ridges are the only routes that can be traversed. Place names are often unusual, either of Indian origin or of typical mountaineer description. One ridge in this region is called "Chunky Gal Mountain." To the east, within another curve of the Blue Ridge, is the spectacular Tallulah Gorge. This stream, with headwaters all around the great curve, flows directly south to Burton Reservoir.

In this section the Trail was often impeded by "blowdowns," trees of various sizes that had been uprooted or broken off by wind storms. Getting over, under, or around these was a tiresome business, but this alone could not account for the fact my strength was waning. At times it was necessary to stretch out on the ground for a few minutes to recuperate or to sit on a tree trunk momentarily while stepping over. Something definitely was wrong. Otherwise the Lone Expedition had settled down, with my feet toughened, my pack streamlined and drawn in at the top for better balance, for easier passage under obstructions, and for better all-around handling.

Arrowheads, found in the "Land of the Noonday Sun," were arranged by the author to form the A.T. symbol.

Low rigging seemed best on narrow side-hill footing and over rocks, as well as uphill. The nagging problem was my growing weakness. It was now a case of shape up or head for the nearest bus or train station while strength remained to get off the mountain.

About noon I stopped at a spring to cook. Considering that meals had sometimes been missed altogether because of rainy weather, I decided to cook a double amount so that some could be kept and eaten cold if no fire was possible that evening. To my amazement the entire kettleful of "sawdust pudding" disappeared like magic, along with half a pound of brown sugar, a can of milk, and some raisins. Almost instantly my legs lost that leaden feeling and I felt like hiking again. It had been a case of starvation pure and simple, despite no unusual sensation of hunger. From that time on my strength increased and so did my food bill.

Fog closed in again as I passed a deserted logging camp and then came to Deep Gap Campground. Because of the dense fog I didn't spot the shelter and started up the switchback trail to the firetower on the summit where a sign said this was Standing Indian, elevation 5498 feet. The view from this magnificent summit, known as the "Grandstand of the Southern Appalachians," is usually far reaching in every direction. Right then it was practically zero. The tower loomed like an embattled outpost defying the overwhelming forces of nature gone mad. Thick gray waves of fog were pouring across the peak in a vaporous flood. The mountain seemed to be tilting away from that raging current. The feeling was much like that in a hurricane.

Not wanting to spend the night under such conditions—the tower was locked and deserted—I scurried down the far slope in the fading daylight, reaching Beech Gap in the deep dark. That definitely was one of the worst nights on the entire trip, no fire and boggy ground underneath. At least no mosquitoes were active, because of the cold wind, no doubt. Naturally my morning start was "soon." At the first stream I tried to cook but conditions were so poor that a match went out before it had burned halfway. About noon I reached a drier spot and managed a meal.

Meanwhile the Trail route had turned north again after dipping almost to Georgia, forming still another Blue Ridge curve enclosing the headwaters of the Nantahala River flowing northward. Actually the water divide trends to the east from this point as a lower ridge enclosing the jumbled uplands of central North Carolina, with literally thousands of "tops" and pinnacles. All the waters within this region of heavy rainfall eventually reach the Mississippi River through deep gorges in the high ridges to the northwest. Many minerals of good quality and quantity are found in central North Carolina and mining is a leading industry. Instead of twisting through these jumbled uplands the Appalachian Trail trends northwestward through the Nantahala region on a dominant cross ridge to the Great Smoky Range. Perhaps in the future an alternate route of the Trail could follow the eastern water divide and eventually cross Mt. Mitchell and Grandfather Mountain before rejoining the A.T. again in southern Virginia. This is the route projected in Benton MacKaye's orginal sketch.

As a whole the mountains of western North Carolina are extremely rugged, including the highest, most jumbled terrain in all the Appalachian System. Between the low east rim and the towering Smokies are high cross ridges and great enclosed valleys, so isolated that for many years each was almost a world of its own. This complex structure was first explored and mapped more than a hundred years ago by a distinguished educator, Professor Arnold Guyot, of Princeton University and originally from Switzerland. His manuscript, "Notes on the Geography of the Mountain District of Western North Carolina," was submitted to the government in Washington in 1863, seemingly for military use in the Civil War. It lay in government files, forgotten until discovered and published in the 1930s. The manuscript was amazingly accurate and contained an incredible amount of first hand information.

Weather improved, the sun shining occasionally as I cruised northward over good trail and came in early evening to Wallace Gap, named, according to local legend, for a man who once fought a panther there with only a knife. While easing myself onto a bank to rest I heard a car coming up a dirt road from the left. It stopped and a large man wearing high leather boots swung one foot to the running board and sat there looking me over. Pinned to his shirt was a big silver badge. Apparently he was puzzled and was waiting for me to make the next move. Weary or not it was time for me to stand up and explain myself. His expression changed when he learned I was trail-hiking. It was Game Protector Buchanan of the Southern District of Nantahala National Forest. He and his son, who was driving, were headed for Rainbow Springs and he said to put my pack in the trunk if I wanted to go to the store. Why he mentioned the store became evident later.

On the winding road downward we passed many abandoned houses. Rainbow Springs was a ghost town, once a logging center, but the timber had run out. It had no post office now but Mr. Buchanan said that mail directed there might have gone to Prentiss, the nearest post office, and I could meet the rural mailman the next day. At the lower end of town were a few occupied houses and a little old store. Outside was a cage containing a big wildcat the warden had trapped. It hissed and spat wickedly when we passed. The store lady offered me a newspaper to read, the first I had seen in nearly two weeks. I sat on a bench by the potbellied stove to read it but put it aside after scarcely a glance. The doings of the outside world no longer interested me. Only the Long Cruise was important now.

Back at Wallace Gap the warden asked where I planned to stay the night. When I shrugged and said wherever I happened to be, he offered to take me down to a campground near his home and bring me back up in the morning. At the campground he gave the boy a long look. The boy glanced at my small hand axe, then trotted off to the house and returned with a double bitted axe, then borrowed my knife, which was more to his liking, and soon had a fire blazing in a fireplace. I peeled potatoes, started them cooking and added the contents of a large can of vegetable soup. Mr. Buchanan said he often made that mixture himself and that it was "good eatin'." Meanwhile a thunderstorm was approaching and he said I might as well stay in the empty Ranger shack down the road. It contained mattressed bunks and a chunk stove, practically a palace by present standards. He and the boy remained to talk until ten o'clock. In one corner of the cabin was a small wall mirror. Happening to glance into it I drew back, amazed. My face was drawn thin, my eyes wide and staring, and my hair gone wild. No wonder he had stared at me so strangely at first, probably thought me a fugitive from the chain gang.

A morning knock on the door awakened me. It was the boy, to make sure I was awake and to start the fire again. Soon a horn sounded. I toted the pack outside then gawked in amazement. Perched on the hood, fenders, and trunk of the old coupe were at least a half dozen kids, leaving the seat inside for me. With such a load the old car was seldom out of low gear all the way to the gap, where they were meeting the school bus. Since the mailman wasn't due until ten o'clock Mr. Buchanan drove me around the town, pointing out the ruins of the big house where the logging boss had lived. He obviously was proud of his Nantahala domain; said he had been promoted to the Dismal Swamp one time but soon transferred back to the mountains. After letting me off at the store he resumed his duties of patrolling the National Forest and trapping predators. The mailman had no letters for me and I prepared to leave. The store lady was disappointed, said she had planned to feed me a big slice of country ham for dinner but didn't insist when I got that faraway look in my eyes and said lots of miles lay ahead and I already had tarried long. A few miles north of Wallace Gap the Trail became narrow and treacherous along leaf-strewn slopes. Footing was uncertain and a slip could mean a long, sliding fall. Reaction in such cases is to sprawl and get as much traction as possible. On rocks the opposite is best, risk arm injury to avoid leg injury. By repeatedly self-instructing for different dangers, the necessary reflexes can be acquired. It's much like programming a computer. Lone travel means high risks and the margin of safety must be increased in any way possible. I've never had a serious injury in a lifetime of hiking, including many work trips, and firmly believe this mental preparation is the main reason.

At Wayah Gap was a picnic area and a trail shelter, a handy place to stop and cook. From there the Trail ascended a winding toteroad, sometimes bordering precipices, to the summit of Wayah Bald, elevation 5500. On top is a massive stone memorial to a man who served as Supervisor of Nantahala National forest for more than twenty-five years. The view is similar to that from Blood Mountain or Standing Indian, panoramic and far reaching. Rain of the previous night was still blowing off and billowy white clouds were casting shadows in shifting shapes on every side. The ridge northward is high and leads to Burningtown Bald, where I decided to stop at the leanto, where washing clothes was logical because of abundant water. Unfortunately, more rain came at night and the clothes didn't dry. But the weather cleared for a while and I swung the clothes around to dry as I hiked, surely a strange sight for anyone who might have been watching.

At noontime the rain had resumed and I was on another long upslope, this time to the firetower on the summit of Wesser Bald. While still a hundred yards from the tower I noticed a man on the catwalk waving and calling, "C'mon up, c'mon up." Says I to myself, "That guy must really be lonesome." He was a typically tall, lean mountaineer and was cooking his noonday meal. Very casually he went about adding to skillet and kettle. Presently he dished out pan bread, spoon gravy, bacon, beans, and coffee and said, "Help me eat this, too much for one." He said he liked the job of lookout fairly well but was a family man and didn't like being alone so much. Just then the phone rang. He listened a moment, then grinned across at me and said, "I got a visitor today, a lone trail-hiker. He wants to take right off again but I won't hardly let him." He explained afterward that his family called from Tellico Valley sometimes to break the monotony but would not call again until he told them I had left.

The weather was rainy but when I talked about leaving he countered with "Better stay the night" and kept up such a constant talking that leaving was difficult. We talked about hunting, politics, war experiences—he had also been in the Pacific—and numerous other topics. He told of a bear hunt the previous autumn with some of his cronies, chasing down a giant black bear with his pack of dogs. It was a running fight, with the dogs getting the worst of it while he was frantically trying to keep them from getting killed or crippled. One of his buddies finally caught up and shot the bear. It took two days to get the bear off the mountain, and the parts they packed out to a store where a scale was available weighed a total of five hundred and three pounds. He said he knew where another "big old bear" hung out and he would take me to the hunt if I came back in the Fall.

At suppertime my host gleefully declared it was now too late to leave, pointed to the extra bunk on hand in case a Ranger stopped by, and reached for the cooking gear. He said this was one of the best towers in the district. It was about fifteen feet square, equipped with chunk stove, wood box, the two bunks, two chairs, telephone, two-way radio, and orientation table. With rain still falling, I wasn't hard to persuade. After supper, talking resumed. At eleven o'clock we agreed it was time to sleep. The silence lasted at least five minutes before he said, "You know, I often lay awake at night and think about most everything under creation." At twelve we tried again with similar results and again at twelve-thirty before we fell asleep.

The light of a clear dawn awoke me. The storm had settled into the surrounding valleys, leaving the highest peaks jutting like islands from a sea of fog. Then the sun rose, lighting a golden path across that misty sea. Seldom, even in the South Seas, have I seen anything to compare. Later the fog cleared, revealing a wild and beautiful panorama. South and west lay a jumbled expanse of ridges with deep valleys between. Eastward was the Tellico Valley, still full of fog. Below to the north lay the canyon of Wesser Creek, descending steeply to the deep abyss of Nantahala Gorge. Beyond, on the skyline, was the silhouetted crest of the entire Smoky Mountain Range, loftiest and most massive east of the Rockies.

During breakfast the towerman grinned and said, "Well, we fought about three wars and four election campaigns and hunted nigh every critter in the woods last evening and I enjoyed every minute of it. Why don't you stay over a day or two? We got lots more to talk about." When reminded that the end of the Trail was far away and time was fleeting he agreed, but while I was packing he kept repeating, "I hate to see ye go, I hate to see ye go."

Part way down the canyon was a small farm, the house of stone, nicely handled and the small fields nearby neatly kept. A man was sitting on the porch, gazing toward the Smokies. I told him I always had wanted a place like this, where no one could build higher up. He smiled and replied, "It does make you feel better." Farther down the

An overshot water wheel was all that remained of an old mill in Wesser Canyon.

creek was an old mill wheel, so ancient it was settling into the bank of the stream. The rest of the mill was already gone. At the juncture with the main road at Wesser was a small ramshackle store, crammed to the rafters with an amazing variety of groceries and other goods. I stopped to get food and to leave the pack while sidetracking to Bryson City for color film, one thing the old gentleman didn't have in stock. He mentioned that another hiker had stopped the day before and he had never seen a hungrier man. This individual, though rather small, had devoured the contents of several large cans, as well as large quantities of cookies and candy before leaving the store.

A ride on a lumber truck got me to Bryson City. Besides color film I bought a small spoon and spatula, which would work much better than my axe for turning pan bread. After all, you can go only so far for simplification. Two short rides then got me back to Wesser, where the Trail crossed the river on the highway bridge. However, marking was entirely lacking and I missed the turn off the road, continuing into the gorge until the mistake was obvious. The choice now was to backtrack or to bushwhack up the steep, high slope, which is what I chose and thereby jeopardized the entire expedition, instead of saving time. The greenbriers were incredibly nasty and the slope almost perpendicular. I must have been a pathetic figure, streaming with sweat, bleeding from scratches, every muscle aching, crawling endlessly in a back-slipping, bush-clutching struggle before coming out on top. While recuperating, flat on my back, I vowed to avoid such foolishness in the future.

The weather chilled that night as I bivouacked in a high gap, where the sound of running water somewhere below guaranteed water for breakfast. Nightwind sounds much the same but moves. Next day I side-trailed from Stekoah Gap to Cheoah to mail home the tent, ridding myself of seven useless pounds. Then the trek resumed along the crest of Cheoah Mountain over a series of "tops" before dropping abruptly to follow a creek for several miles, criss-crossing back and forth on corduroy roadway, which is made by placing logs or poles crosswise. By now the sun was low but I kept on in hope of reaching a shelter. For once it worked. In the deep dusk I rounded a spur and spotted a leanto in the next cove, then spotted a man as he stepped outside. He was the one who had started from Oglethorpe on Easter Sunday. His buddy had joined him at Wesser. They planned to hike until time for college in the Fall, hoping to go all the way.

The first one said he had tried to start from Katahdin but was stopped by Rangers. I was to hear details of this later in Maine. He left Millinocket in early March through foot-deep snow, wearing riding boots and carrying an enormous pack. Luckily two game wardens on a snow sled—driven by an airplane motor—crossed his trail, followed, and found him sitting in the snow and about to fall asleep, permanently. They hustled him back to town and told him to come back in June. Instead he caught a train for Georgia. He and his buddy were using Mountain Troop framepacks, same as I was, but had not stripped them down for efficiency. Their footgear was tennis shoes for dry weather, rubber hightops during rain, a combination guaranteed to ruin the toughest feet.

While I was cutting wood one of them said in an undertone, "Look at that! He's cutting more wood in five minutes that I did in an hour." At bedtime he said he would set the alarm clock for an early start because they wanted to reach the Smokies the next day. Sure enough, the blare of that mechanized rooster, a full-sized Big Ben, shattered the sylvan silence at five-thirty. At daybreak they departed, noticing I was awake and remarking that I probably would be overtaking them anyway, which I did about nine o'clock. Just how eccentric they really were soon became evident. Both carried binoculars and cameras and stopped to inspect closely birds, animals, bugs, rocks, flowers, trees, whatever. Everything was discussed at length, without any background knowledge; they kept no records and reached no conclusions. The mental picture I retain is of one holding a salamander by the tail while the other photographed it.

Marking was extremely poor. When we came to a trail junction overlooking the village of Fontana Dam we didn't know which way to

The Smoky Mountains formed a backdrop for this view of Fontana Dam, from a vantage point no longer on the A.T.

go, so decided to ask in town. No one seemed to know, but our maps, such as they were, indicated a continuation on Yellow Creek Mountain to Tapoco. Actually the Trail was being changed to cross Fontana Dam but the marking had not been changed. So we continued on Yellow Creek Mountain. Fontana Dam is part of the Tennessee Valley Authority and one of the highest dams in the world. The workers lived in the village which now had become a resort center for vacationers and fishermen.

All afternoon we plodded along the crest of Yellow Creek Mountain over a series of upthrust peaks, made treacherous by steep and leafy slopes. Sometimes lizards skittered from underfoot, keeping us careful and thinking of snakes. My companions had been medical corpsmen in the navy. One planned to be a research scientist and the other one a naturalist, which explained their intense interest in flora and fauna. We discussed hiking gear and the light loads they were carrying, about thirty pounds each. I recalled seeing a toothbrush along the Trail in Georgia. "Hmmm," says the guy, "thought I heaved that into the brush." My toothbrush, by the way, was not thrown away but it did lose its handle. Inevitably, a long-distance hiker must choose between traveling light and not traveling at all.

Tapoco is a small resort town at the juncture of the Cheoah and Little Tennessee Rivers. As we approached the end of the ridge overlooking the town, conditions became so bad that we lost the

Trail completely. We finally bushwhacked down that brushy mountainside, and no better word could be found to describe that sliding, crashing descent. The other two headed immediately in the direction of Tapoco Lodge, a deluxe tourist haven, as if they couldn't wait to escape the forest, while I was loathe to leave its solitude. I never saw them again. After shaving at the riverside—it was my policy to be as presentable as possible—I headed for the grocery, which someone told me was a mile away on a side road. The place was typical, little more than a shanty, but locked and deserted. A man at a nearby house said the proprietor was "up the road a piece" helping to roof a house. Eventually he came and opened for business. The only thing he could find to put my stuff in—customers brought their own containers—was an old potato sack, so up the road I went with it over my shoulder. Had anyone suggested that gunny sack would go with me all the way to Maine I surely would have called him crazy, but it did, proving useful in many ways, one of my best accoutrements.

No mail was waiting at the post office but the postmaster gave me a map of the Great Smoky Park, showing the Trail route and shelter locations. For the next few days I actually would know the names of places and what to expect. All my life I had wanted to see this Mecca of mountain fanatics, the land of the soulful song. The ex-navy men were nowhere in sight as I stowed my grub in the pack and moved along. Half a dozen young folks were standing at the bridge. They stared curiously but said nothing. The Trail turned upslope on a dirt road toward the Park. The sun had already dropped behind the ridge.

The past two weeks were vivid memory now as I trudged along. The trailway through the Nantahala had been extremely rugged and is in fact considered to be one of the most strenuous parts of the entire Trail route. This is because of the up-and-down travel over a series of cross ridges. But the weather had improved greatly and I was hitting my stride. During those two weeks it sometimes had been difficult to persuade myself to keep going. How easy it would have been to quit. But the mood was changing. Now I would have had to be dragged off the Trail. I had come to the woods to walk with Spring. Says I to myself, "Get going, Ridgerunner! Remember that song you wrote one time far off in the Coral Sea. . . ."

> *A whisper comes in the dead of night*
> *When lonely stars are shining,*
> *The restlessness of a bird of flight*
> *From deep within me pining.*
> *From lonely seas to the mountains high*
> *I'll roam the whole world over,*
> *A vagabond of the wind and sky,*
> *For I was born a rover.*

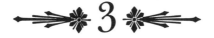

3

Alone with the Sky

Walking by moonlight on top of Old Smoky,
Up on the grasslands, alone with the sky,
While down in the deeps of the shadowy valleys
Wistful and wild is the whip-poor-will cry.

TAPOCO, at an elevation slightly below two thousand feet in Deals Gap, is the western gateway to the Great Smoky Mountains National Park. A nearby dam across the Little Tennessee River forms Lake Cheoah, the backwater extending almost to Fontana Dam. Both are a part of the system built by the Tennessee Valley Authority. The concept of "source to mouth control" of the Tennessee River watershed was originated by Benton MacKaye. His chart of the proposed plan hung for more than twenty years in the headquarters of the Forest Service in Washington before the TVA was begun in the thirties, and he spent several years in the actual planning. He had worked under Gifford Pinchot in the planning of National Forests during Theodore Roosevelt's term.

Elevations on the Great Smoky ridge are often more than three times as high as Deals Gap and other nearby points. This difference of three to four thousand feet between ridgetop and valley floor accounts for the impressive aspect of these magnificent mountains. The sudden upthrust from the Tennessee Valley causes the abundant rainfall, some of the heaviest in the country. Plants grow to enormous size. One of the largest trees ever found in eastern United States was a tulip poplar in the Nantahalas of North Carolina that measured over 20 feet in circumference. Mountain laurel and other shrubs grow to the size of small trees.

Before reaching the Smokies I had imagined them as a fearsome place of rocky crestline, little water, and few trail shelters. Actually this lofty range is one of the easiest A.T. sections to hike, even though it is the highest. According to Guyot this is the dominant ridge of the Appalachian Highlands, yet the top is amazingly level and the footing seldom rough. Maintenance is by the Park Service, including a chain of leanto shelters.

Breakfast was late at the Moore Spring Shelter on Gregory Bald. The shelter has since been dismantled, and the A.T. relocated from the site.

The weather was turning cold and windy as I climbed from Deals Gap, and a brilliant moon was shining when I stopped to sleep. With poncho underneath and the pack to windward, I rolled in the blanket and pulled the gunny sack over my feet. Meanwhile those ex-navy guys undoubtedly were sleeping in so-called luxury at Tapoco Lodge. I fell asleep to the lullaby of the wind in the trees and the somewhere calling of a whip-poor-will. Most people never in all their lives sleep under the open sky, and never realize what they are missing.

The first tall peak next day was Parsons Bald, elevation 4948 feet. Beyond were the high meadowlands of Sheep Pen Gap and then the open summit of Gregory Bald, almost a mile high. Near the edge of the timber were Moore Spring and the nearby shelter, built of logs and split shakes. I paused there to cook a belated breakfast. From this peak a side trail leads down Gregory Ridge to Cades Cove, one of the most historic places in all Appalachia. A few Cherokees still lived there when settlers came. According to a popular legend, the name evolved from "Katy's Cove." As the wife of the local chief she was matriarch of the tribal group and therefore symbolic owner of the land.

The settlement in Cades Cove remained isolated for nearly a hundred years, until establishment of the Great Smoky Park. Some of the homesteads and other original structures have been preserved or restored for visitors to see. Some of the descendants of original settlers remain. Construction was mostly of logs, dovetailed

Patches of wildflowers, like this bed of spring beauty in the Smokies, sometimes extended for miles "so thick they couldn't be avoided, even on the footpath."

The roof of the Spence Field Shelter appeared in a high ravine. Close up, food and supplies abandoned by others created an eerie mystery.

together like antique furniture. At least a hundred square miles are encircled by the mountains. Trails lead to the high "balds" where cattle were grazed and crops such as cotton or corn were grown.

Weather was perfect during the afternoon, so warm I could have gone barefoot. The blazing sunlight was blistering my nose but also was burning away the lingering effects of the early struggle through fog and cold rain. My strength was building up from the low ebb of the second week and my hopes were soaring. Some people suffer from high elevations but the mile-high level is where I come alive. Flowers were blooming everywhere. Dogwood and other shrubs were plentiful but the greatest display was on the ground. Sometimes one patch extended for miles, so thick they couldn't be avoided, even on the footpath. Violets, spring beauty, bluet, Jack-in-the-pulpit, and may-apple were numerous. It is said that more flower species are found in the Smokies than in any other area of the same size on earth. People usually come when the rhododendron or azaleas are blooming but the myriad ground flowers in April and May on the far back places are the botanists' delight. And everything is extra large.

Once, while resting against a small pine tree, as the tufted branches discouraged a horde of gnats, I noticed a spoon lying in the grass. It was stainless, definitely superior to the one I had bought in Bryson City, so an exchange was made. This is my "Smoky spoon," which will be gladly surrendered to anyone proving ownership. At Spence Field Campsite, one of the highest east of the Rockies, and consisting of a spring in a clump of rhododendron and many acres of grassland on the ridge crest, I paused to cook, then rambled on. A full moon was rising and Spence Field Shelter was only a few miles ahead. Moonlight enhances the majestic solitude of the Great Smokies, softening distant objects into luminous unreality. All was serene, with the cool thin air a pleasant tonic perfumed by countless wild flowers. Tall dead grass from the previous year crunched crisply underfoot. The bordering trees were barely beginning to leaf. Only a breath of breeze whispered along the crest that night and only the brightest stars showed through the sheen of moonlight.

My steps were a weary stumble when the roof of the shelter appeared in a high ravine. Shaded from the overhead moon, the interior was black but the brilliant light revealed extraordinary details out front. Rustic tables were loaded with a variety of canned goods, jars of jam or butter, other jars of "fatback" or ham, enormous pancakes still in the skillets, and plates of partially eaten food. Was the shelter full of people? Yet there was absolute silence. I struck a match to look. The leanto was empty. Here was a mystery indeed but I was already more than half asleep and morning would be soon enough to solve the puzzle.

Even then, by daylight, the place had an eerie look, something like a ghost town. Apparently a party had come for the weekend and then left in the middle of a meal. Cans and other litter were strewn from here to yonder. Amongst the rubble were several empty whiskey bottles, mute evidence of what had caused the exodus. I cleaned up the mess somewhat, then rewarded myself with a liberal breakfast from the abandoned supplies. Next was Thunderhead, tallest peak so far at 5530 feet. Views were far reaching, over the Trail just hiked and to the Tennessee Valley westward. Farther on, the path followed a narrow crest with views over Tennessee to the left and North Carolina to the right. Then came an aisle of shrubs bearing bell-shaped blossoms.

People often complain of encountering rainy weather in the Smokies, of storms that come with little warning, strike with terrific

With Tennessee on the left, and North Carolina on the right, the A.T. route followed the narrow crestline boundary of the two states.

force, and disappear just as suddenly. I wouldn't know. For me it was four straight days of sunnytime and moonlit nights, a halcyon interlude. The only drawback was the chronic sunburn that resulted. At Silers Bald Shelter in mid-afternoon I decided to stop early and catch up with chores. The main project was to cut the blanket to mummy shape and sew on a long zipper that had been filched from the tent. My change of clothing was washed and dried. The pack was checked over and further modified. This was the final "shakedown" and no important changes were made during the rest of the trek. As usual before turning in I scribbled the day's impressions in the Little Black Notebook. On such a night it is so easy to stare into an ember fire, while thought is free as wind in the trees or water among worn stones.

So far the timber had been mostly hardwood, some of the largest remaining in the United States. The third day brought dense evergreen forests, mostly spruce and fir, known to the mountain people as "he-balsam" and "she-balsam." These trees are tremendous for upland growth, some towering above a hundred feet, and with base diameters of two and a half or three feet. They stand so close and the canopy is so thick that little sunlight reaches the ground. When an old monarch uproots or breaks off it often is caught and held partially upright by its neighbors. In such a forest primeval it is fitting to sing the old mountain song, "In the pines, in the pines, where the sun never shines." The Smoky Park was set aside primarily to preserve such remnants of the mighty forests once growing in this country.

National Park designation has checked exploitation to some extent but fire is more difficult to control. One area had been completely denuded by a blaze that started far down a steep ravine and burned to the ridge crest, a sight almost as depressing as a battlefield. Such fires usually result from carelessness, a match, a cigarette, a campfire left smouldering, and the restless wind does the rest. The people who start the fires often do not realize what they have done. The same kind of carelessness causes enormous destruction of buildings and loss of life.

Clingmans Dome, once known as Smoky Dome, is the highest summit in the Smokies, and the highest point on the Appalachian Trail at 6643 feet. It is the second highest peak east of the Mississippi, the highest being Mt. Mitchell, which is about forty feet higher. On Clingmans Dome I came to the massive log observation tower—since replaced by a modern tower—and climbed topside to get pictures. Another shutterbug was there and we discussed the views. Then two couples arrived, so well groomed that I muttered about looking so rough. One of the men smiled and said that was how a hiker should look, adding that his store sold the same brand of boots I was wearing. As I left they bid me "Good Luck and Happy Trails."

The heavy stand of fir and spruce that crowns Old Smoky extends all the way through Indian Gap, where the Cherokees crossed to the Overhill Towns in Tennessee, to Newfound Gap. The Trail winds through this area of ancient trees, which still are thriving. All phases of the life cycle are present, from tiny seedlings through the sapling and mature stages, to the overage monarchs that soon will join the great moss-covered ancestrals already moldering into the forest floor.

Looking back toward Silers Bald (from the south slope of Clingman's Dome) where the aftermath of a forest fire provided a sight "almost as depressing as a battlefield."

Newfound Gap is the hub of tourist traffic in the Great Smoky Park. Cars and buses were parked around the traffic circle and people were everywhere. Nearby is a memorial to the Rockefeller family, which donated part of the money to establish the Park. Other funds or land donations came from Tennessee and North Carolina. Near the memorial was a large lady wearing a sun suit and leading a

Ogles Market was a shopper's paradise. It also happened to be the only store then in Gatlinburg, Tenn.

small boy by the hand. She took one look at my brick red face and blistered nose and laughingly declared, "I like sunshine but not that good." Somehow she reminded me of the lady that first day in Georgia.

After getting as shipshape as possible in the comfort station I caught a bus for Gatlinburg, Tennessee. Two drivers were aboard and the sight of me started them talking about bears. They mentioned every instance they could recall of people getting mauled or bitten. When told that I carried no gun one said he reckoned the best policy was to run anyhow. Actually bears can be very dangerous in the Park because they are half tame and not afraid of people. Because of the early season I hadn't seen any.

In Gatlinburg I dashed across the road from the bus station to Charlie Ogle's Store, a combination of supermarket, sporting goods store, and general store. The sign said, "We Sell Everything." A bus in the opposite direction was due in a few minutes so I bought some groceries in a hurry and didn't linger in this shoppers' paradise. This bus driver was interested in snakes, and he had plenty of time to elaborate while ascending the winding road, including the loop where the highway crosses itself. He described fatal and near fatal encounters with rattlesnakes and assured me they could really strike their entire length. He too regretted my lack of a gun. As I was leaving the bus at Newfound Gap he drawled, "Well, take it slow and easy now, Buddy." The other passengers looked very sympathetic.

The westward views from Charlies Bunion were spectacular, but glances downward were horrifying. Fire had stripped the rocks of any growth along the steep ledges.

On the North Carolina side of the Park is Qualla Indian Reservation, home of the Eastern Band of Cherokees. These are descendants of tribesmen who managed to escape the "Trail of Tears" and hide in the Smoky wilderness. They bought the land through a white agent, then had it taken from them again before it was finally established as a reservation. One of the Cherokee leaders was Sequoya, inventor of the Indian alphabet. He was a leader in the attempt to have the Blue Ridge loop become the state of Cherokee, a plan that enraged land-hungry settlers. Tribal hero is Junaluska, who gave himself up to be shot so that his people might remain in the Smokies.

A few miles east of the Newfound Gap is Charlies Bunion, an appalling place. Years ago a forest fire burned the area to the bare rocks. The Trail follows a narrow ledge, with a long, sheer drop below. The view westward is spectacular. The view downward is horrifying. This section, known as the Sawteeth Range, has a crest so narrow that the footway is sometimes buttressed with rocks. At nightfall I was between shelters and decided to push on to Hughes Ridge by moonlight. While moving along, sometimes in the open, other times through hardwood forest where the moon cast intricate shadows upon the forest floor, I thought of my old-time buddy, lost in the war. Part of a letter he wrote when we were in different parts of the Pacific came back in vivid retrospect: "Remember the shadows we cast on water 'twixt sunset and sunrise, like panning for gold, or something lost. But we do walk on the same trails of thought." Was he walking with me now, in spirit?

At Camel Hump Mountain in the Smokies, the Trail was narrow, along a steep slope buttressed with rocks.

Because of freezing temperatures that night at Hughes Ridge I bedded down in front of the fireplace and kept a warming fire. The trick is in being able to wake at the right times during the night to replenish the fire. It's also prudent to keep water handy in case of flying sparks. A better idea is to carry a warmer bedroll in the first place. Squirrels were barking and chipmunks scurrying in the morning. The Trail led on through dense evergreen forest, the trees tall and slender in the reach for sunlight. The path was gullied by heavy rains and logs had been placed to divert water flow. Occasionally a vista would open westward to spacious farmlands in Tennessee. At Tri-Corner Knob Leanto, one of the best in the Park and with one of the coldest and sweetest springs, a sign had been fastened to the crossbeam by District Ranger Ralph Shaver urging hikers to keep the area neat and to be careful with fire.

The Trail route skirts the summit of Mt. Guyot, second highest peak in the Park, and the side trail was obscure and obstructed by fallen trees. Like Clingmans Dome, this peak does not have an open summit. At Camel Hump Mountain the Trail turns abruptly over a ledge, opening a vista toward Mt. Sterling, on the right. Three pictures were taken here, each one distinctive. One was through a blooming "sarvis" tree toward the Big Pigeon Valley and another was of the Trail turning left along the steep slope, buttressed with rocks. From there the path turned downward gradually, then steeply down a ravine, and finally through a backyard and along a walk to the road in Davenport Gap. My tryst with Old Smoky was over. But the memories live on. Nowhere else on the Appalachian Trail do I feel so strong an urge to return.

Mountain Medley

A medley of summit pastures,
spring flowers and whip-poor-wills,
Stone churches and upland rivers,
and steep farm-sided hills.

THE VALLEY OF THE BIG PIGEON RIVER, coming out of the Blue Ridge loop, is the highest and most rugged of the watershed basins of the Southern Appalachians. It is bounded on the southwest by the Balsam Mountains, described by Guyot as "by far the most massive and continuous of all the transverse chains—among these it may be called the master chain, as the Great Smoky, its close neighbor, is the master chain of the longitudinal ridges." The A.T. crossed the Big Pigeon River on a cable bridge at Waterville, a bridge that swayed and rocked as I ventured over. On the other side were the buildings of a small farm. Marking was vague and I was fumbling around near the barn when a man hailed me from the porch of the house, insisting I "come and set for a while." His name was J.L. Moore. When told I was from Pennsylvania he insisted I surely knew Dick Lamb, who was from Philadelphia. Dick had knocked on the door one rainy night and begged for permission to sleep on the porch. Mr. Moore promptly insisted he sleep in the guest room, and now proposed that I do the same. I tried to decline with thanks, the time being midafternoon, but Mrs. Moore joined him in insisting, "Ain't anyone like you gonna sleep on the mountain when we got a perfectly good extra bed." The Moores were talkative and kept on till midnight, one of their favorite subjects being Dick Lamb. He still wrote to them occasionally. I was to hear more of him months later in Vermont, and finally met him several years later.

Mr. Moore wakened me at 5:30 A.M. to one of the most elaborate breakfasts imaginable. Mrs. Moore must have been up at least an hour earlier. Included were hot biscuits, corn bread, fried ham, fried eggs, bacon, spoon gravy, cereal, jam, butter, cow's milk, goat's milk, and probably more. Half an hour later, when I could hold no more, Mr. Moore ushered me out the door, saying he knew I was anxious for an early start but to come back as soon as the trip was

The old cable bridge across the Big Pigeon River at Waterville "swayed and rocked as I ventured over."

finished and stay at least a week. Lots of talk and food but very little sleep! I didn't know whether to laugh or cry. His last words were a hearty "Luck to ye."

From Waterville the Trail slanted upward to Snowbird Mountain, with the path overgrown and marking poor. At the top near a large tree five woods roads come together, with no indication of which way to go. Straight ahead led down into hill farm country and several neglected farms. At the second one a seedy-looking man told me I had probably gone astray at "Spanish Oak." Returning there I tried all the roads before finding the right one. Marking beyond was so faint and the route so disrupted that the only way to proceed was by dead reckoning—keep compass in hand for frequent checking and head "thataway." The book method of compass navigation is useless in dense woods.

Marking resumed near Max Patch Mountain, a great grass-covered knoll where a herd of cattle was grazing. The sound of scuffling children, the scolding voice of a woman, and the blaring of a radio came from a weather-beaten house. Beyond, along a dirt road were other houses that seemed to be abandoned. At dark I was still on the road, trending northward but unsure of the way. The moon was rising so I cooked supper by a spring and continued through a region of farms in hope of finding a good place to stop. But slopes got steep and the valley home lights flickered out one by one. Then the road turned abruptly through a gap at a boundary sign between Pisgah and Cherokee National Forests. It was time to stop regardless. The only spot flat enough was above a giant tree stump overlooking the road. Once in the wee hours I woke to see the waning moon high overhead.

My hunch was right. The Trail turned along the state line over a grassy knoll and soon came to Walnut Mountain Shelter, which would have been most welcome the night before. At least it provided a place to cook breakfast. Beyond were brush and grasslands, then a section of recently logged timber. Roads had been bulldozed all over the mountain and guesswork was necessary again. The shambles ended and the Trail resumed near Hot Springs, approaching town at the District Forest Service Headquarters. The man on duty looked me over and said, "You must be that lone trail-hiker we've been hearing about." Apparently the man on Wesser Bald had passed the word. From this time on for more than five hundred miles, to the northern end of the Shenandoah National Park, the Rangers and Wardens kept track of "That Lone Trail-hiker," and offered to do whatever they could to help.

The Appalachian Trail passes through Hot Springs to cross the French Broad River. This beautiful stream drains one of the largest enclosed valleys of the Southern Appalachians, reaching past Asheville and almost to the state line of South Carolina. The highest headwaters are from Mt. Mitchell. No color film was available in Hot Springs but the stores had plenty of food. The Little Black Notebook says that three and a half dollars worth was purchased, and "my aching back." Even half a dozen eggs were included. Fresh food would be eaten first, then back to staples like cornmeal, oatmeal, brown sugar, and raisins. One advantage, more or less, in backpacking is that when you have less food for strength you also have less weight to carry.

Beyond town I stopped to talk with a boy sitting on the porch of an "outway" house. His mother soon came out and told some of the local history. She mentioned a white-bearded old man who stayed for a while in an old hut on the mountain, then quietly disappeared. Another man, also bearded, had lodged in town and also roamed around studying flowers and birds. Farther up the ridge the trailway was narrow along steep slopes. When dark closed in the only flat place for sleeping was on the Trail itself. Placing a pole on the outer side to prevent rolling off, I bedded down but slept badly, thinking a deer might come around the sharp bend in high gear. Another disturbing factor was a whip-poor-will that kept flying back and forth and calling — calling — calling. Its nest must have been nearby.

The leanto that should have been reached was only a mile beyond. Talkin' when I should have been walkin' obviously had thrown me off schedule. But just seeing the leanto and having a good place to cook breakfast cheered me so much I was singing one of my vagabond ditties at the top of my voice when, suddenly, the silence was deafening. A moment later came the clink of metal on stone. A root digger was about a hundred feet away, plying his trade with mattock and gunny sack. His working had silenced the birds and my singing had silenced him. A few minutes later, as we talked, his two sons resumed digging nearby, startling me again. They had kept perfectly motionless and unseen until convinced I was friendly, a typical trait of such mountain people. The man said he "liked the mountains real good" and often stayed out for weeks at a time. He said he had killed a rattler with thirteen rattles and a button a few days before but that it was early for them to be "crawlin'." He feared copperheads the most, putting it this way, "A rattlesnake's a gentleman, he'll sing and let you know he's there, but a copperhead just lays there and lashes out at ye."

At Deep Gap I stopped at the roadside restaurant for a change of diet. Adjoining was a store run by a man who originally was from Pennsylvania. He insisted I corroborate his claims about the many whitetail deer in the Keystone State. Leaving my pack there, I ventured out to Greeneville for color film. Getting there was easy, a delivery man had stopped at the store. Returning was totally different. The baseball season was opening and everyone on the road was headed for the nearest diamond, or else was going fishing. Plenty of walking and three short pickups finally got me back. One driver was the proprietor of a gas station at the foot of the mountain. We discussed the upcoming presidential election. He thought Dewey would make a good President—probably was one of the people interviewed by Gallup.

From Deep Gap the Trail slants upward several miles to Camp Creek Bald. Ed Tweed, the fire lookout, was a veteran of eleven years on the Camp Creek Tower. He said the Ranger at Hot Springs had radioed about my coming through. Just then the phone rang. He listened, then winked in my direction while answering, "Yeah, he just pulled in, must have missed you because of the logging mess over your way." It was the towerman farther south, on the torn-up mountain.

Like the tower on Wesser Bald, the Camp Creek Tower was well equipped and Ed insisted I stay overnight. By now I knew that the lookouts get lonesome and like to have congenial visitors. Ed told of a time the previous year, soon after he came on the tower, while snow was still on the ground, when he was below cutting firewood. He heard a roar on the next "top," followed by a scream like a woman in mortal agony. Next thing he knew he was scrambling up the tower. Then an animal, "tall as a yearling heifer," came by within a hundred feet of the tower, screaming and roaring by turns. Next morning he found tracks as big as his clenched fist. At one point the animal had stepped over a knee-high log without brushing snow from the top. It had to be a mountain lion, rare in the Appalachians.

My sleep that night was troubled, but not by cougars. About midnight I wakened, as though it were dawn, but it was only the late moon shining through the many windows. Ed said he was bothered the same way. Otherwise the windows were fine, providing panoramic views. By day the city of Greeneville was plainly visible and the lights were brilliant at night. On the ridge eastward was an open "field," used during the war as an emergency landing strip. Like the man at Wesser, Ed was reluctant to see me go. Two hours later the Lone Expedition came to Chestnut Log Gap, where an abandoned cabin stood at trailside. Upslope was a fine sweet-water spring. The mood was on me and this is what I scribbled:

> *Along the eastern line of Tennessee,*
> *High in a gap with vistas either way,*
> *The old log cabin fascinated me*
> *While passing by one sunlit April day.*
> *One end is tumbledown. The chimney stands*
> *Half sundered from the once snug-fitting wall,*
> *Long since neglected of its builder's hands,*
> *An aura of decay pervading all.*
> *Who built this lofty home along the Trail*
> *So long ago and chose the site so well?*
> *If these old logs could speak what rustic tale*
> *Of plans and hopes and toil would they tell?*
> *Reluctantly I leave, for here there seems*
> *To be fulfillment of somebody's dreams.*

Hardly a cloud was in a bright blue sky as I moved along over a ridgetop pasture land and came to Big Butt Mountain, elevation about 4900 feet. There I saw a grave, with head stones for Wm. Shelton and David Shelton, killed in a skirmish during the Civil War. Someone keeps the grave site clear. Believe it or not, as I turned away the clarion call of an eagle sounded overhead.

Though northward bound, the A.T. trends southward from Big Butt, coming down to Devils Fork Gap. Beyond was rugged hill country, with many steep slopes cleared for farming or grazing. John Fox, Jr., author of the folk classic *Trail of the Lonesome Pine*, must have meant such terrain when telling of a man who fell out of his corn field and broke his leg. Fences were plentiful, more crossed in one afternoon than in all the previous hiking. Each was a major hurdle, consisting of a pyramidal style rail fence grown thick with briers, and usually reinforced with barbwire. Testing each strand of wire or weathered rail in turn, one must inch carefully toward the summit, then descend the far side, trying to avoid the almost inevitable catastrophe when something breaks and drops the intrepid backpacker upon rails, briers, and wire. I dubbed this "The Brier and Barbwire Country."

According to the Little Black Notebook, my feet began hurting during the afternoon. I bathed in a stream, reached a road crossing at dusk, and stopped by a spring in a pine woods nearby. Traffic was

"If these old logs could speak what rustic tale/Of plans and hopes and toil would they tell?" Already abandoned by 1948, the trailside cabin in Chestnut Log Gap no longer exists.

heavy, this being Sunday evening. I felt a little lonesome, so near and yet so far from everybody. The next day brought more briers and decrepit fences and then a high grassy knoll. The view from topside was definitely springtime. Surrounding valleys were snow-white with dogwood. On the back trail were the hill farms I had crossed so laboriously. Beyond the knoll were brushy grasslands, with the weather turning windy and cloudy. Finding the way became difficult, with marking faint and mostly on rocks. Cattle trails in every direction were confusing. Once a pair of scarlet tanagers appeared ahead, flashing red as they flitted through the trees, keeping just far enough ahead to prevent pictures. The tanager is one of the shyest and most beautiful of all songbirds.

Toward evening the Trail entered forest again, some of it rhododendron-grown to the size of small trees, with trunks at least a foot in diameter. Then, abruptly, the path dropped into the gorge of the Nolichucky River at Unaka Springs. The 'Chucky, as it is affectionately known to local people, is a beautiful stream flowing west to a juncture with the French Broad River in Tennessee. Its headwaters also come from the Mitchell area but from the opposite side of the mountain. According to legend, one of the earliest settlements

On Big Butt Mountain were the graves of two cousins killed during the Civil War.

of the Cherokees was in the beautiful valley of the Nolichucky. My camp that night was in Lost Cove, near an abandoned house near the river. Whip-poor-wills came so close their eyes glowed red in the firelight and their calls were deafening. Scribbled in the Little Black Notebook is the following:

> 'Chucky Blue
>
> By the River Nolichucky,
>   Streaming by in brimful flow,
> When the shadow shapes move darkly
>   In the fading campfire glow,
> There's a face appears before me
>   Of a girl I'll someday know,
> With her lips half smiling shyly
>   And her lashes drooping low.
>
> Then the forest seems to murmur,
>   With a voice in every tree
> By the shore of 'Chucky River
>   By the hills of Tennessee,
> And I seem to hear her whisper
>   This melancholy plea,
> "Whither art thou, Forest Rover?
>   Will you ever come to me?"

Fire had scarred the top of Unaka Mountain. Nature tended her wounds, however, and the area is once again dressed in green.

From the Nolichucky Gorge the A.T. followed a side valley to Curley Maple Gap, and then the open crest of Unaka Mountain. An outstanding viewpoint is Beauty Spot, an unusually scenic bald with panoramic views. Much of Unaka Mountain had burned more than twenty years before, leaving many thousands of acres of desolation. Sometimes no more than blackened rocks and charred stumps perched on taproots remained. Thickets of briers were the only new growth. Marking was almost nil. Once I started on a beeline across some tedious switchback, more suitable for pack animals, but turned back to the road when a large blacksnake slithered from underfoot. A sign at the top mentioned Rattlesnake Ridge. Once while crossing a gap where trees still grew I saw smoke ahead and expected to encounter a forest fire, but it was a man and a boy burning brush while clearing an area for pasture. The same day I recall seeing a buzzard rise ahead and found the bones and shriveled skin of a blacksnake that must have been at least ten feet long. Finally the burned area merged with sprouts and then a remnant of pine forest in a ravine leading down to the village of Limestone Cove.

At a grocery store the man was familiar with the Trail and pointed to a battered sign on a fence post across the road. He was amazed that I had gotten this far without guidebooks. On down the road at another store a customer said the Trail followed the Simerly Creek Road but some said it followed the ridge top. I chased that ridgetop rumor and spent the night under some pines, then wandered around on various "roads," about four feet wide, through old-style hill farms. It was like stepping back a hundred years. The fields were incredibly steep and rocky, causing me to wonder how anyone could make even a meager living on such tip-tilted terrain. At one place a man was loosening ground with an old bull tongue plow. Turning down one of the sledge roads, I came to a little old schoolhouse, where the road widened to wagon size. It was recess time. The youngsters acted as though they had never seen a man carrying a pack. All playing ceased while they lined up along the bank to watch silently until some of the girls began to titter. That stretch of road seemed mighty long.

Farther down was Simerly Creek Road, which I should have followed in the first place. A few minutes later a teenage boy on a bicycle overtook me and slowed alongside. We talked as though we had known each other for years. After several miles he said, "Well this is where I live," turned into a yard, said, "Well, be seeing you," then turned to glance back and add in a low voice, "Though I know I never will." The memory of that parting, after so brief an acquaintance, has haunted me ever since.

Near Hampton I stopped to shave with water from Simerly Creek. My boots had worn very thin and I hoped to find a cobbler in town, and did. He half-soled my boots while I lunched on cookies and milk obtained at the grocery counter in the same building: I wanted to try walking without heels, as the Indians did, so told him not to replace them. He finally agreed but joined the growing list of people who doubted my sanity. He, and everyone else in town, seemed to know nothing about the Appalachian Trail, not even that it went through as indicated on my road map. I started northward at the crossroads and passed the site of Watauga Dam, then under construction, with heavy equipment on all sides. Upstream the land had been cleared to water line and hundreds of families were moving out. A grocery and service station was still operating and I stopped for information, suspecting the Trail lay beyond the long, high ridge to my left. The proprietor conferred with several customers, then reckoned a trail went up the mountain but no one knew what shape it was in. But all agreed there was an old cabin part way up where I could stay the night. Rain began falling as I started off.

At the foot of the mountain a man coming out of a house said he was just visiting friends and didn't know about the trail, then added with a sardonic grin, "That's a mighty big mountain you're headed for, son." A pall of cloud closed in, and the trail faded at the old cabin, which was padlocked. Sleeping on the ramshackle porch was damp and drafty but far better than the rain-drenched woods. In the morning I tried desperately to bushwhack upward, knowing the crest must be no more than a quarter mile away, but it was hopeless. The man at the store agreed and for an instant only I contemplated another try. Meanwhile the store stove was roaring hot and I kept turning to dry out evenly.

Later on, as the rain was easing, a delapidated car stopped for gas and the driver agreed to carry me back to Hampton. I wondered whether the old bucket of bolts would last that far. Most of the windows were gone, replaced with cardboard. Most of the upholstery was missing and at least two cylinders were not firing. He made room in the back for me and the pack, amidst jutting coil springs and tattered fabric. Then he stopped at a rural barroom along the way for beer and slot machines. The machine was jammed several times as he fed it nickels but always unjammed after the bartender whacked it with a chunk of wood he kept handy. The bartender shrugged in disgust when I ordered soda. Later we rattled and lurched into Hampton, where I thanked the man emphatically, then started west from the crossroads. Soon a road branched north and a battered sign indicated the Lone Expedition was back on track after a full day lost in the hinterlands.

Later, as I hurried along, a car approached from the rear. It was Rev. Lloyd Greer of Damascus, Virginia. We talked a bit and then he offered up a prayer for my well-being and the success of my long trek. A few hours later he came by in the opposite direction and stopped to tell me to write him to let him know how I was getting along. The sun finally came out as I reached Watauga River, this time on the proper side of the mountain. Near the bridge, in a rapids, was an oldtime undershot water wheel, probably used to irrigate the nearby bottomlands. Farther along were a settlement and a small schoolhouse, behind a wire fence. A car came along and stopped, letting off a young lady who turned toward the schoolhouse, probably the schoolma'am. The gate, a typical southland type consisting of an extra post secured by two wire loops, seemed to be stuck. She glanced helplessly in my direction. Unfortunately the local Pecks Bad Boy must have jammed that gate, and getting it open was an embarrassing struggle. At the grocery store a small dog came yapping and nipping ferociously until called off by the storekeeper. I bought the only jar of honey in stock, so old the man didn't know how much to charge for it. He said most everyone had their own "gums" and didn't buy store honey.

Watauga Valley has quite a history. It was one of the earliest settlements of Scotch-Irish who had migrated south from Pennsylvania and displaced the Cherokees. When English and Indian forces invaded the area during the Revolution, the settlers banded together to win the Battle of Kings Mountain, the decisive battle in the southern mountain region, under the leadership of John Sevier. The Watauga Settlements declared independence and had a written constitution long before the rest of the country. Daniel Boone and Davy Crockett ventured west from Watauga Valley.

A major relocation now takes the Appalachian Trail east of Hampton through the beautiful Laurel Fork Gorge, with its large waterfall, and over spectacular Roan Mountain. To the east is

An oldtime undershot water wheel, probably used to irrigate the adjacent bottomlands, stood near a bridge across the Watauga River.

Grandfather Mountain, visited by the naturalist Michaux and described by him as "the highest Mountain in all America." It rises high from valley level but not that high.

The old route continued up Watauga Valley, finally turning into timberland. Marking was good and I hastened on, looking for shelter, and came to a small ramshackle leanto. Rain began and the roof leaked but the most unfortunate thing about the shelter was the mouse that peeked from a cranny. I was forewarned but thought the pack would be safe next to my head. The little rascal was bolder than expected and managed to chew a hole in my waterproof bag, leaving souvenirs in everything, including the salt. Most of my supplies had to be thrown away. Now being in haste to reach a store I covered at least twenty miles on Holston Mountain and finally slept in a Forest Service shed at Maple Springs. The night was windy and cold and I rose at dawn to hurry the few remaining miles to Damascus, over in Virginia.

The nomad life of the woods had now become my routine existence. I had come a total of four hundred and twenty miles, averaging about sixteen per day. Only a serious mishap could stop me now. The Long Cruise was well under way.

5

Storm Camps and Pinnacles

People and creatures and wearisome miles,
Storm camps and pinnacles . . . How will it end?
Somehow the joys seem to balance the trials
Found in the future around the next bend.

THE APPALACHIAN TRAIL crossed from Tennessee to Virginia a
few miles south of Damascus, approaching the town through a grove
of tall pine trees. I stopped at a gas station to get a road map and at a
grocery store for supplies. A May Day celebration was in progress, a
carnival in full swing.

On the far side of town the Trail slanted up a long ravine to the
crest of Iron Mountain and came to Feathercamp Firetower. The
towerman wasn't surprised. He had heard I was coming through.
Southward loomed Mt. Rogers, highest peak in Virginia at 5719 feet
elevation, and nearby Whitetop, almost as high and easily recog-
nized. Between them is an alpine area similar to parts of the Smokies.
The Trail has recently been relocated through this area. The warden said he had spotted a "smoke" beyond Whitetop where North
Carolina, Virginia, and Tennessee meet in a zigzag line; he had to
get a cross bearing from another tower to determine which state the
fire was in.

My stop that night was farther east at a spring near Skulls Gap.
A thunderstorm was threatening but it went down a side valley and
the morning weather was perfect. Once a long black stick, supposedly, moved and became an eight-foot black snake. Herds of
cattle were grazing, usually with a giant bull presiding, and these had
to be detoured. Even a bear or a mountain lion will not attack such a
monster.

Pasture lands continued all day, with marking poor, and camp
was pitched in a clump of pines. The night was windy and cold, and
an early start brought more pastures. Breakfast was cooked at an
abandoned cabin, which gave protection from the wind. A firetower
in this district had a large "No visitors" sign, which was scrupulously
obeyed. Many rail fences crisscrossed the grasslands during the
afternoon. Dry camp was pitched under pines after dark.

This grove of pine trees has now been replaced by pasture land where the A.T. approaches Damascus.

Morning brought rain and a farming community, and a man burning trash. This was C.S. Jackson, retired after long service in the U.S. Forest Service, and the man who had first marked most of the Trail in the Holston District. He had been in charge of a CCC crew fighting a stubborn fire on the ridge I had followed the previous day. He spoke of the fine crop of hay on his farm, stacked in the usual way, in conical shape around upright poles. Farther along I caught up with a tall slow-talking and slow-walking individual and stayed with him until the trailway turned up Farmers Mountain, overlooking Byllesby Dam, on the New River.

This stream is one of the oldest, geologically, in the world and certainly one of the most unusual. Its highest headwaters are in North Carolina, near Roan Mountain. It trends northeastward into Virginia, then gradually veers westward into West Virginia, cutting through the Alleghenies in the deep, long New River Gorge. Its waters eventually flow into the Ohio and Mississippi Rivers and empty into the Gulf of Mexico, completing more than two-thirds of a circle. It is the last of the Appalachian rivers to break westward, out of the Blue Ridge loop. Rivers farther north rise in the Alleghenies and break through the Blue Ridge to the Atlantic Ocean.

The Trail turned southward along the railroad and New River for about six miles to Fries Junction. Waiting for a train in the station was a man who said he had been bitten by a "spreadhead" years before, but reached a doctor within fifteen minutes. The sickness that resulted recurred every year during hot weather and he believed the poison remained in his body. Other snakebite survivors have since told me the same thing. Spreadhead apparently is a local name for cottonmouth moccasin.

Evening brought heavy rain. No one in Fries seemed to know anything about the Trail. One man said a ferry operated to Galax but not this late in the evening. The storekeeper said he was closing but I could be out of the wet at his place across the street while deciding what to do. He then insisted on providing supper, consisting of ham, spoon gravy, and other leftovers, which tasted mighty good to a famished hiker. He then drove me around by road to Galax, where I was able to get a room in a tourist home. This was my first night spent indoors since the Moore home at Waterville and marked the end of my first month of hiking, and also a distance of about five hundred miles, the right progress for a trip all-the-way. This fact, along with a good night's sleep and clearing skies in the morning, restored my cheerful outlook.

My map indicated the Trail route going southeast to the Blue Ridge Parkway so I followed roads in that direction and intercepted the scenic highway near the North Carolina line, a few miles north of Grandfather Mountain. The Parkway follows the eastern Blue Ridge, in this region a plateau with its eastern rim overlooking the Piedmont. The A.T. cut back and forth across the newly built Parkway along the old "Ridge Road," with marking no more than a trace. Toward evening I met a farmer and asked the distance to Galax. He said about twenty-five miles. By sundown I must have gone at least thirty, the longest day's walk of the entire trek. The point of total exhaustion was near. The road was flanked mostly by fields but I finally came to a patch of woods and turned aside. That night I dreamed of a path that moved underfoot like a treadmill, so rapidly I lost ground instead of gaining.

In the morning I came to Puckett Cabin, along the Parkway. This hewn log structure was the home of "Aunt Arlene," who traveled to hundreds of isolated cabins as a midwife. Meanwhile she had twenty-four children herself but none lived past infancy. She died at the age of one hundred and two. I was following the Parkway now because it had taken over the Trail route. Flame azaleas were in full bloom along the roadside, together with dogwood and many species of ground flowers. Visible to the east was Pilot Mountain, a massive pinnacle jutting from the Piedmont.

By now I was weary of road-walking. Abruptly came an interruption. Veering eastward, the Trail came to a deep, wild gorge. Jutting from the bottom of that steep walled canyon was a peak as

The A.T. routing across the Pinnacles of the Dan had started as a joke. The views along this rugged section of Trail were spectacular.

pointed as a pyramid, its top reaching the level of the canyon walls. Did the Trail actually cross that incredible peak? It did, descending through a sag, then up and over the pinpoint summit. It was rock work pure and simple, with a precipice on either side. Yet rhododendron grew from crannies and the air was fragrant with their blooms. Any pack at all, much more the forty pounds I was carrying, was a handicap and even a hazard. The view from topside was astounding, with the Dan River so close on three sides that it seldom could be seen because of intervening trees. On the far side it was necessary to go backward most of the time, along narrow ledges and clutching bushes to keep from falling. Marking was close together and very necessary. Wading the river was next and then the ascent of the "Indian Ladder," up a sheer cliff grown solidly with rhododendron. This couple of miles was probably the most rugged and most spectacular segment of the Trail, which now has been relocated far to the west. This incredible peak is called the Pinnacles of the Dan, and is visible from the Parkway.

The story of how the Pinnacles of the Dan came to be a part of the Trail was told me years later by Charlie Thomas, one of the most loyal and most eccentric of all the "Headquarters Gang." Charlie and another oldtimer were on a trail scouting trip with Myron Avery. Captain Avery was farther south, marking and measuring. They decided to play a joke on him by pretending to route the Trail over the Pinnacles, expecting him to reject the idea. Instead he climbed the peak, was impressed with the view, and approved the route. They might have known. He always favored the scenic way, rather than ease of access.

More road-walking followed the break at Pinnacles of the Dan and heavy rain began falling. At dark I was forced to stop in a rain-drenched woods. A fire was essential. Instructions for fire starting sometimes say, "find a mouse nest." It is much more practical to make one. Pick the tiny twigs under evergreen trees, laurel bushes, or other resinous growths, and crush them into a ball. When held over a lighted match this ball of fine twigs will ignite, whether wet or dry. Then bigger and bigger twigs are added. I gathered firewood, still carrying the pack lest it be lost in the darkness, and set up a pole and poncho shelter, facing west away from the rain. About midnight a clear-up storm roared in from the west, collapsing the shelter. I broke up the pole frame for wood to keep the fire burning and huddled under the poncho until the rain stopped, then hunted more poles to erect a windbreak. That was a night to remember, or try to forget. I remember the twinkling stars.

Morning weather was after-rain, foliage shining in the sunlight and new growth scenting the air. Suddenly the feeling of eyes upon me brought a halt. To the right was a fox, sitting in silhouette upon a knoll. While I remained motionless it stayed but with my first step it wheeled away, the sunlight glistening on its gray fur.

By midday the weather turned rough again, with a gusty northwest wind and sleety rain. Later I learned this squall was caused by a severe storm in West Virginia. While fighting this wicked headwind I noticed a farmer plowing in a field, with a team of two mules and a horse. He waved, then halted the team in mid furrow, and came over to the fence, a most unusual action for any farmer, especially in the South. He said his name was Handy, adding, "I ain't got no eddication, that's why I'm followin' the plow, but I like to talk to everyone as sensible as I can." Mr. Handy didn't lack "eddication," just "book larnin'." He owned two hundred acres of farmland, and a hundred acres of pasture and rented another tract, starting from scratch as a young man. He had built a large new house to replace the little cabin in which he and his wife had started out. He invited me to go along with him to eat, saying, "My wife's in the hospital for an operation but my girl's comin' over from her place to make somethin'. If she don't come we can cook up a snack ourselves." Ordinarily, I would have declined with thanks but somehow this was different.

Mr. Handy resumed plowing toward the far end of the field with me walking alongside and recalling the days when I had worked on farms and did some walk-plowing myself. Then I noticed a young man by the fencerow ahead. He was moving around aimlessly, as though he could not keep still. Mr. Handy said, "That's my boy, got throwed, shellshocked, that is, in the army. I got him home from the Veteran's Hospital. Maybe it'll do him good if you talk with him." When Mr. Handy introduced us the boy hardly seemed to notice, clutching the back of his neck as though from pain or numbness.

Mr. Handy unhitched the team and told the boy to take the horse, which belonged to him, across the meadow to the barn and feed it while he took the mules to an outlying shed to fetch a load of hay. I walked along with the boy and asked him the age of his horse. His voice was hardly more than a whisper when he said "Two year." Those were the only words I ever heard him speak. At the barn he fed the horse while we waited for his father to arrive with the hay cart. Suddenly a strange thing happened. He took off his corduroy cap, set it on my bare head, and stepped back to see how it looked. I got out my floppy rainhat, my only headgear, and set it on his head. That made him laugh a little.

Mr. Handy soon came in a hurry, just ahead of a rain squall. We unloaded the hay, then went to the house, where his daughter had indeed come and made "a little somethin'." Included were fried ham, spoon gravy—made from the fryings—stewed apples, goat's milk, and real southern cornbread, the kind that is broken, not sliced. We talked at least an hour. Mr. Handy said I should stay the night, "or a week for that matter," but I told him the Spring weather was moving north and I was going along. He agreed that this was logical but it took another half hour to get away. For a man whose wife was in the hospital for an operation and whose son was almost

The Dale Mabry Mill was once the center of activity in a mountain community. This site, along the Blue Ridge Parkway, is far from the present A.T. route.

hopelessly shellshocked, he was remarkably cheerful. He said that Meadows of Dan were about "three short miles" away. My estimate was more, but the icy rain squalls may have been a factor.

At the store I bought supplies, then stood by the pot-bellied stove to warm up. The storekeeper recalled a shelter at Rocky Knob, a few miles up the Parkway and I determined to reach there if possible. Weather was clearing as I soon came to Dale Mabry Mill and stopped to take a picture. In the old days this was the center of activity in the mountain community, including grist mill, sawmill, and cider press, along with the nearby wheelwright and blacksmith shops. The wheel was about fifteen feet high, overshot, and fed from a long wooden spillway. The area is maintained by the National Park Service as a historic point. I finally stumbled into Rocky Knob by starlight and found the shelter was of stone, open on three sides and with a cold wind howling through. I gathered some snags for fireplace wood and a sackful of leaves to cushion the stone floor. The temperature must have been around freezing.

The morning view from Rocky Knob showed the Piedmont eastward, studded with pinnacles. Within this vista, about ten miles away, is Fairystone State Park, where the tiny cross-shaped luckstones are found. Near the pavilion was a metal A.T. marker and marking continued for about a mile but faded in the middle of an overgrown field. I headed back to the Parkway.

A cold night wind howled through the stone shelter at Rocky Knob.

Half an hour later a Park Service car stopped and District Ranger Bill Lord offered a ride. When I declined he stayed to talk a while. He had heard about me at the store in Meadows of Dan. We were discussing the flower display along the Parkway when two elderly ladies stopped to admire a bush of azaleas. Bill said he hoped they didn't try to pick any and force him to take action, but they only admired and soon were gone. Bill had been to Europe during the war and had since gone back to visit in Switzerland. As we talked the "Smoke Chaser" assigned to that section of Parkway came by and also stopped. Patrols like his were necessary because people often threw burning cigarette butts or matches from cars and caused grass or brush fires. He said, "It's not guys like you we worry about. You know how to handle fire. It's the picnickers who make fires where no water is available and the drivers who don't use their ash trays." Concerning rattlesnakes, a favorite subject, he said they really could strike their own length, rising from the coils before striking forward.

Later I began to count steps, checking against mile markers, and found my original estimate of two thousand per mile to be about right. This is true of fairly level terrain. Steep uphill requires about twice as many and steep downhill even more, something like changing gears in a truck. On the basis of this an all-the-way hike over the Appalachian Trail requires at least five million straight-ahead steps.

The campground at Smarts View included comfort stations, drinking fountains, fireplaces, and picnic tables. Prominently displayed as a historic structure was Trails Cabin, similar to Puckett Cabin, and said to be the last of its kind built. The floor was dirt, the walls unchinked, and the fireplace of field stone. It is said that pioneer mountain people were never satisfied without two things, plenty of good water and plenty of fresh air. Trails Cabin certainly provided the latter. My bed that night was in front of one of the picnic fireplaces, to allow a warming fire. Voices somewhere indicated other campers but I didn't see them until morning. It was a middle-aged couple who said they had wintered in Florida and now were on their way to summer in Maine. What a rugged life! Later, while shaving in the comfort station, I marveled that they had even spoken to such a wild-haired and whiskered individual. Since it was Sunday I tried but still must have looked unusual. Sightseers stared at me as much as at the scenery.

At Pine Spur two men were setting up a movie camera. I shied away lest they judge me suitable for a wild man from Borneo role. Dozens of people were on the overlook, admiring the view. I felt detached from them, like a stranger in a far country. Northward the A.T. was sometimes traceable next to a parallel dirt road, along which I came to a store. A man lounging in front asked about the Smokies, which he had visited several times. He told of a man who went into the bush for as long as six months at a time and people thought he was only a woods bum. Actually he was a government man scouting the Park Trail System.

At Bent Mountain the Trail definitely parted from the Parkway, beginning the wide swing around Roanoke. My bed that night was in a woodlot behind a church. Dogs in the vicinity sensed my presence and barked frequently all night long but no one came to investigate or evict me. A dawn start took me along a ridge and then a long ravine past summer homes to the village of Glenvar. Noticing a small restaurant and being more hungry than usual, I entered and immediately classified the proprietress as Irish and amiable. When I specified onion with my hamburger she said, "How about tomato?" I replied, "Sure, give it everything." It came rigged like a Dagwood Special. The lady laughed at my expression and said, "Well, you said give it everything." At a nearby store the clerk said the only bread they had was "salt rising," which "takes a little gettin' used to." He was right but the texture and flavor were excellent. He said the Trail passed an abandoned cabin near the top of the ridge but too far away to reach before dark. But a campsite could be found along a stream on the way up, information that proved to be correct. Mosquitoes were troublesome for the first time, meaning that repellent and netting would be necessary from now on.

The store clerk was also right about the cabin. It was small, about four feet high in the front and sloping to the rear, probably a shepherd's hut. The roof was mostly gone and some of the logs rotting, but the view was wonderful and a sweetwater spring was nearby. Marking was bad and I soon went astray, coming on a woods road to a gate and a sign too weathered to read. Assuming it concerned vehicular traffic, I ventured on and came to a group of buildings, spotted what looked like a dwelling, and knocked on the door to ask about the Trail. The door immediately flew open and a small man with a furious expression began to revile me harshly, declaring I had willfully encroached on a wildlife refuge, demanding my name and address, and threatening a lengthy jail term. After a second or two in shock I tried to explain but seemed to make no impression. After all this time and effort it appeared that the Long Cruise would come to an ignominious end in the local hoosegow. But he finally simmered down and even allowed me to get water from the spring before taking the shortest route out of the sanctuary. Verily, "a soft answer turneth away wrath."

The map showed the Trail crossing Route 311 near Salem so I followed woods roads in that direction, finally arriving at the town. The post office had no mail. The sporting goods store had repellent but no netting. I finally got some by asking in a department store, getting flimsy black stuff that undoubtedly was stylish. Back at the Trail from the road crossing, I came to Catawba Mountain and started up in the twilight, came to a waterfall and bedded down on a flat place just beyond reach of the spray. All night long the waters sang their soothing lullaby.

In the years since 1948 most of the Appalachian Trail between Damascus and Roanoke has been changed. Beyond the relocation over Whitetop and Mt. Rogers the Trail turns northeastward and follows the crests of a number of long, high, wooded ridges in southwestern Virginia. From one such crest there are views into Burkes Garden, from another into West Virginia. Thus the conflict with the Blue Ridge Parkway was eliminated but also eliminated were such points of interest as the Pinnacles of the Dan. Perhaps in the future an alternate route could be restored to the eastern Blue Ridge, from Grandfather Mountain north, even if some stretches had to follow the Parkway. Pinnacles of the Dan alone would make it worthwhile, not to mention Grandfather and Mitchell.

About one-fourth of the Appalachian Trail is in Virginia, much more than in any other state. Most of it is now in National Forest, eliminating the road-walking that was so tiresome in the past. At the time of the Long Cruise the decision to relocate had already been made, actually before the war, which explains the confusion I encountered. The result was my hit or miss passage along the approximate route.

From Catawba Mountain north most of the relocations resulting from the Parkway construction had already been made, even though some parts of the scenic highway had not yet been built. The terrain was different and such a drastic move as the one in southwestern Virginia was not necessary. As in the Shenandoah farther north the Trail would cross the "tops" while the Parkway would swing back and forth through the gaps. This is the only way a foot trail and a highway can share a mountain range with any degree of compatibility.

The middle of May is a fine time to be in the Blue Ridge Mountains of Virginia, moving north with the Spring. On top of Catawba Mountain I came to a large cherry tree on which was a "Prevent Forest Fires, It Pays" sign. Just then a half-grown woodchuck scrambled up the back side and perched in the fork long enough to be photographed. On the far side of the mountain another 'chuck whistled as I passed an abandoned house. Its burrow was under the foundation. This farm had been a beauty spot, with flower beds and trellises everywhere. Now wild flowers and weeds were competing with remnants of cultivated species and rows of neglected berry bushes. The wilderness was taking over. Against a bank were ripe wild strawberries, the first ones on the trip. The lure was irresistible. Not even a thicket of greenbriers can stop me as effectively as strawberries.

Another rain storm began as the Lone Expedition came to a high ridge studded with outcroppings, sometimes forming overhangs. Hiking became a hectic affair of dripping poncho, slippery rocks, and sloshy feet. This lasted for several hours to a four-lane highway at Cloverdale, north of Roanoke. I stopped at the service station and grocery for supplies and to stay out of the wet for a while. A man who stopped for gas stared at me a moment, then declared bluntly, "Man, there's nothin' in this world would get me into the woods in this weather and into such condition. Where you gonna stay tonight?" When told "In the woods somewhere," he shook his head very sadly.

That's exactly what happened. At dark I spotted the top of a logged-out pine, draped the poncho over two jutting limbs and began cutting off other limbs beneath to make room and to provide firewood. It wasn't my best bivouac, but not the worst one either. Pine will burn under such conditions, and the smoke discourages mosquitoes. The Little Black Notebook says that supper was spaghetti and biscuits and that I didn't sleep much. But the rain vanished late and stars peeked through before disappearing into the dawn. The Trail then turned along roads through a residential district. The weather was fine and my happiness must have been showing. A girl waiting for a bus smiled—or laughed—and a few minutes later two more did the same. Then a gang of youngsters at a crossroads watched me approach and cheered when I turned the right way.

By midmorning the Expedition came to the Parkway, under construction north of Roanoke. A work crew was cutting and filling

North of Roanoke, ongoing construction of the Blue Ridge Parkway provided curious sightings—first, bulldozers, and then, a wild turkey.

with bulldozers, power shovels, and a fleet of trucks. I spread my gear to dry on a bank and sewed my boots, which were loosening at the seams. The truckers coming by stared so intently they almost ran off the road. At the head of construction, which was obliterating the Trail, I had to circle to get ahead. Toward evening the Parkway appeared again, finished except for black-topping. Once a wild turkey crossed ahead. At twilight I dry camped on top of a knoll, with Peaks of Otter looming northeastward.

Bearwallow Gap was only a mile farther and I stopped there at a roadside spring to cook breakfast, using a twig fire. I was repacking when a Forest Service truck came up and stopped. Once again I heard, "You must be that Lone Trail-hiker." It was Ranger Jim Luck. He insisted on driving me down a side road to see a mountainside covered with blooming rhododendron. Ranger Jim was very proud of his territory around Peaks of Otter and persuaded me to go that way, even though the Trail had been recently changed to bypass it. Later he walked with me up Sharp Top and pointed out the "local curiosities," Turtleback, Needle's Eye, and Buzzard's Roost. To the north, across a deep notch, was Flat Top, higher by several feet but less spectacular. The peaks got their name from the stream between, where Indians once trapped otter.

According to Cherokee legend the peaks were the northernmost part of their range at the time of the Jamestown settlement. In *Myths of the Cherokee,* James Mooney tells of white men who visited the Indians and wrote accounts for English journals. These twin peaks are said by some to jut higher above valley level than any others in the Appalachian Chain. Ranger Luck said he was one of the men flown to Maine to fight the disastrous fire at Bar Harbor the previous year. When one of the crew asked if he had ever been in a

The firetower on Sharp Top yielded new friends, views of the other Peaks of Otter, and some unexpected food. The tower is no longer on the A.T.

plane before he said yes, figuring the firetower on Sharp Top was practically the same thing. Suddenly he interrupted himself to point down to a line of cars slowly ascending a switchback below. He decided this must be a professor from Lynchburg College and his students on a field trip, which proved later to be correct.

Meanwhile the towerman was preparing to leave, this being May 15 when the fire season normally ends. He offered me a half pound of bacon and a small can of beans he still had on hand. I accepted gratefully, being almost out of supplies and knowing the next store was at least two days away. He and the Ranger waved from the catwalk as I left. On the road below the summit I met the caravan. The driver of the first car asked if I was trail-hiking, then introduced himself as Professor Ruskin S. Freer, of Lynchburg College, and also president of the Natural Bridge Appalachian Trail Club. He and his students talked with me about an hour and one of them snapped a picture. After that the trek resumed and I came to Apple Orchard Mountain, and the relocated Trail. The only apple tree was wild, and in full bloom. The surrounding valleys were white with dogwood, state flower of Virginia. Dinner was cooked by the firetower, with water from the cistern, and consisted of pan bread and the can of beans. My drycamp that night was on the top of another peak, my favorite place to sleep.

In the morning I cooked more pan bread to go with the bacon, then began a forced march to Snowden, on the James River, where I hoped to find a store. Rhododendron was in full bloom and laurel was budding, some of it so tall and heavy it might be classed as trees.

About noon I reached a point overlooking the James River and turned down the spur toward the bridge, just below the power dam. People were fishing in the backwater, one a plump individual munching a sandwich. My stomach growled. A car was leaving and I asked about a lift. The driver, D.E. Powell, of Bedford, said he actually was headed the other way but would take me anyhow, adding, "I've never lost out yet by being sociable."

Snowden was mainly one building, in which were the post office, the store, and the residence of the proprietor. The store was enough for me. Only two things are more necessary to life than food: air and water. On the way back Mr. Powell said I was to send him the rattles if I ever killed a rattlesnake. My camp that night was by the firetower on Bluff Mountain, and my supper was substantial. Breakfast was ditto. The Trail slanted down to Pedlar Dam, where dozens of people were fishing below the spillway. The Trail crossed a rickety foot bridge that creaked and swayed but delayed its final collapse until some less fortunate, or less starved, individual attempted to cross.

Up the valley were two more fishermen, one of them the nephew of the keeper of the reservoir. No one else seemed to have any luck but they had caught two crappies and a perch. The Trail followed the stream above the reservoir and emerged to a region of high pasture, with hundreds of grazing cattle. Trail blazes were painted on giant boulders or on cairns of stones. At dark I reached a steep, heavily timbered slope and made what later was dubbed my "Guard Rail" camp, done by placing a log or pole above two trees and leveling the space above, then padding it with duff and leaves. A soon start in the morning, no water, took me to the summit of Rocky Mountain, where I got a picture of parallel ridges, with cloud fog between, toward the sunrise. On the far slope was a good spring, where I cooked an oatmeal breakfast, with plenty of raisins and brown sugar. Nearby were many Jack-in-the-pulpits.

During the day the Trail became so faint that finding it became difficult. It seemed to fade altogether near a large domed rock. Climbing topside to look ahead, I found a depression that held a lake in miniature, in a colorful setting of moss and sprouting foliage. In the distance loomed a massive mountain called "The Priest," now crossed by the Trail. Later I learned that this section was being relocated and about seven miles were still missing. Beyond the rock dome the path was faint, then faded altogether at a board sign with an arrow chiseled into it pointing northward. The lack of choice was obvious: start bushwhacking. With compass in hand I battled through greenbriers and other thickets. Suddenly, I heard a sound, unmistakable even to those who have never heard it before. A rattlesnake was "singin'," coiled a few feet ahead of where I was about to step. Once again, as with the wildcat in Georgia, something cold poured along my spine. Backing away slowly, on the lookout for others, I cut a long stick before coming back. I do not believe, as some people do, that poisonous snakes, even in the vicinity of a trail, should not be killed. Too many times I have been too close to being bitten. This one was about three and a half feet long and had ten rattles and a button. Except for one small copperhead, this was the only poisonous snake seen on the Long Cruise. The generally cold and rainy weather must have been a factor.

Two more hours of strenuous bushwhacking then brought me to a blacktop road and the A.L. Hatter grocery store. Both he and Mrs. Hatter were enthusiastic about my trip, which meant a session of talking. She even presented me with a large slice of chocolate cake as I was leaving. Since the evening was moonlit I walked several miles along the road toward the ridge crest before stopping. My supper that night was a large can of spaghetti, another of vegetable soup, most of a loaf of bread and a jar of jam, as well as the chocolate cake. That sounds like gluttony, but a day or two of short rations on a strenuous trip creates a mighty hunger. It's undereating that can be serious.

Next morning I reached and followed a dirt road paralleling the Parkway. A man in a station wagon stopped to offer a lift and was definitely antagonized by my refusal. Then a school bus came by and some of the riders waved from open windows while others hung out to stare. This road soon intercepted the Parkway, which I followed to Humpback Mountain Overlook. A young couple was sitting in a car there, giving the impression they were honeymooners. The man said, "Howdy," so I stopped to talk. Mention of the Trail brought on a discussion as to the proper pronunciation of Appalachian. The lady, who spoke with a Deep South accent, used the pronunciation derived from the Appalachee Indian Tribe, the original source. The man, definitely a northerner, said she would think so, coming from the South where, "They always mess up the language." I agreed with her but didn't say so.

That pesky rain was falling again by the time the Lone Expedition was approaching Rockfish Gap, at the southern end of the Shenandoah National Park. A government car stopped and the driver looked over at me, hunchbacked under my dripping poncho and rainhat, then offered a ride. My refusal brought a quiet question, "What's the story?" He was G.Y. Carpenter, an engineer on the Parkway Project, and a personal friend of Ross Hersey, editor of the *News-Virginian* in Waynesboro. He said that Ross was "very keen" about such things and surely would be happy to see me. Since Waynesboro had been designated as a mailing point I said I would think about it. He said he would call Mr. Hersey in the meantime.

My camp that night was by a spring below the Parkway, with a poncho shelter and fire for drying purposes. In the morning I hid the pack in some blueberry bushes near the Parkway beyond Rockfish Gap, then hitched a ride to town. The girl at the post office handed me some letters, the first received on the trip, then said, "Mr. Hersey called and said to come right over." Says I to myself, "Why not?" Mr. Hersey acted something like a kid on a picnic and afterward detailed photographer Bill Alwood to drive me back to Rockfish Gap and take pictures there. The resulting article and a picture appeared the following day on the front page of the *News-Virginian*.

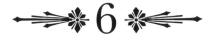

6

Shenandoah

*The charms of Shenandoah
are its foaming waterfalls,
its legends and its vistas
and its geologic walls.*

THE SHENANDOAH NATIONAL PARK is especially valuable because
it is located near densely populated areas of the East Coast, yet is
high and wild and picturesque. The city of Washington is only about
fifty miles away. The Skyline Drive allows thousands of people to
visit the Park as motorists, but a network of trails also allows
backpackers and afternoon hikers to reach the back country. The
Appalachian Trail, which was there first, crosses the high summits
while the roadway swings back and forth at gap level. The unique
topography of the Shenandoah Range makes this compromise
possible.

My side trip to Waynesboro had taken most of the morning.
Before I could get away from Rockfish Gap, a patrol truck stopped
and Ranger Pete Johnson greeted me by name. He too had heard
about that Lone Trail-hiker. We talked almost an hour in friendly
fashion. He said the shelters would be plentiful, a welcome change
from the scarcity since New River. He gave me a fire permit before
leaving. The weather was sunny as I hurried off, to make up time,
and I managed to cover the twenty miles to Black Rock Shelter. The
first seven miles were high pasture land outside the Park, then more
of the same, still retaining some traces of the hill farms once located
in the "hollows."

Black Rock Shelter was nicely built of stone, near a good spring.
In the morning I was yodeling a Jimmie Rodgers song at the top of
my voice when a grouse hen suddenly fluttered ahead. Stopping
instantly and looking at the ground in front of my feet, I spotted tiny
chicks hiding among the leaves. The mother edged closer, ruffling
her feathers like an angry cluck. The chicks panicked and scattered
in every direction, cheeping in terror, while the mother hen practically perched on my toe, a striking example of a wild mother in
defense of her young.

*Traces of hill farms nestled in the "hollows" were visible from the Trail as it
wound through the Shenandoah National Park.*

Soon the Trail broke out of timber to more grassland and a cold
headwind chilled my face and hands. The panoramic views were
much like those in the Smokies. Once again I marveled at the growth
on the crests of the Southern Appalachians. Farther north this
would be timberline. I was resting on a bank at Simmons Gap when
another Park Service truck came up and District Ranger Hopper
introduced himself, having heard about me from Pete Johnson. We
were discussing wood ticks, which were becoming a problem, when
Pete himself came up. He said that three girls had started from
Waynesboro to hike to Waynesboro, Pennsylvania, but were on the
road thumbing the first day and he had driven them a few miles so
they could stay at a shelter. He said I was moving too fast to meet up
with them, despite their hop and skip methods.

Ranger Hopper remained to talk longer, telling of a man rock
climbing ahead of him who had carelessly put his hand within a few
inches of a sleeping rattler. When informed of this afterward and
shown the rattler, he almost fainted from shock. On an adjoining
hillside were the buildings of a hill farm, home of an old mountaineer couple. The Ranger said they would be delighted to keep me
overnight and feed me the "Real old-fashioned mountain food."
This was a temptation but would mean delaying a half day. I had
written my family about meeting me the last weekend in May and
didn't want to risk missing the rendezvous, so I settled for a picture
of the farm.

A patch of strawberries delayed me again just beyond Simmons Gap but I finally reached Hightop Leanto, on a western slope, just as the sun was setting behind Massanutten Mountain in the Shenandoah Valley. The colors were brilliant, from smoky to bright red, and then to blue-green. The wind blew cold so I slept at the fireplace, using the poncho as a windbreak, but didn't manage to keep warm enough to sleep very much. A shelter facing west isn't much good except in hot weather. My thoughts wandered back to the curious shapes the clouds had taken during the day. One looked like a football, one like an aircraft carrier, and another like a drawn out layer cake.

Waiting at Swift Run Gap in the morning was Ranger Hopper, with a copy of the *News-Virginian* containing the story. Before leaving he introduced me to the manager of Swift Run Tavern, who insisted on giving me breakfast. While eating I glanced over the write-up, which included one of the pictures taken at Rockfish Gap and a long column. Some of the copy included questions he hadn't thought to ask. One such excerpt reads, "I asked him how he goes about finding springs and his eyes twinkled as if he was the only one who knew where the gold mine was and said, 'Oh, I just stumble on them.'" The comeback to that was easy. I mailed a card to Editor Hersey informing him I used a peach stick.

In the year 1716, long before the Revolution, Governor Spotswood of the Virginia Colony led a party of men he called "The Knights of the Golden Horseshoe" on an exploratory trip across the Blue Ridge, probably at Swift Run Gap. A commemorative plaque has been placed there, and the highway is called the Spotswood Trail. This expedition did not result in a westward movement of settlers, probably because of the difficult terrain. The western slopes of the Blue Ridge and the Shenandoah Valley were populated mostly by way of the valley southward from Pennsylvania. A Jesuit priest had already drawn a chart of that area as early as 1632.

Through warming weather I traveled on, with Lewis Spring as my objective, and passed the shelter at Bear Fence Mountain, even though a thunderstorm was brewing. That was a mistake. The storm struck with unusual fury in late afternoon and conditions became so bad, with visibility almost zero, that I followed the Skyline Drive from Bootens Gap. During the worst of the downpour a car came by and stopped. When their offer of a ride was declined the occupants left without waiting for an explanation. By the time I reached the next Trail crossing the rain had eased and the woods were bright with a ghostly shining as I slogged through the wetness to reach Lewis Spring Shelter long after dark. My fire wouldn't burn properly and the damp cold penetrated my blanket bag. This was one of the many times when I regretted not bringing a down sleeping bag. Yet keeping one dry enough to be effective would have been almost impossible. Plastic was not available then. Next day a man from

Baltimore told me the temperature at his home was forty degrees. On the mountain it must have been at least ten degrees colder.

East of this area are the headwaters of Rapidan River, which flows between Fork Mountain and Doubletop Mountain. Along the stream and reached by a few miles of side trail is Rapidan Camp, favorite fishing retreat of former President Herbert Hoover. The camp is so close to the river that the President was able to fish for trout from the verandah. Shenandoah Park was then in the process of development.

At Big Meadows the lodge and the restaurant were not yet open but the service station had snacks and a few staple items available. According to the Little Black Notebook my breakfast was peaches and bread. Big Meadows is a sprawling campground about midway of the Park. Farther along I turned aside to Dark Hollow Falls, leaving the pack behind as usual. The pitch was steep and keeping my equilibrium without the pack was difficult. My feet didn't want to reach the ground. That pack had become a part of my natural balance.

Coming back up I met Robert Lamm and his father of Reading, Pennsylvania. They said they often hiked the Trail near that city. Back on the A.T. I was singing "Rose of Tralee" when rounding a bend and came upon a family of three. When I apologized for the racket they smiled and then walked and talked with me until they turned back toward the Drive.

Hawksbill, elevation 4049, is the highest point in Shenandoah Park. The summit is on a loop trail between the A.T. and the Drive. This peak is topped with red spruce, more suitable to the north woods, the same species also found at high elevations in the Smokies, the Mt. Rogers area, and West Virginia. Shenandoah Park contains the northern and southern limits of various plants, providing a variety of specimens almost as great as the Smokies. One difference between the two parks is that the Smokies was mostly virgin timber while the Shenandoah had been settled by hundreds of families and is now reverting to wilderness.

The Trail goes through Skyland, a resort at the southern end of Stony Man Mountain, the second highest point in the Park at 4010 feet. Grazing there at trailside was a fine looking bay horse, obviously someone's prized mount, well groomed and geared with a western saddle and a lariat coiled on the pommel. Just beyond were the stables, where a man was painting the wheel of an old carriage. He said the horse was trained for trick riding and belonged to Mr. Lewis, proprietor of the riding academy. As we talked a group of colorful riders came from the corral and Mr. Lewis joined them riding the bay. The roustabout got them to pose for a picture.

Afterward, Ranger L.Y. Berg approached. He also had heard about me from Pete Johnson. Ranger Berg offered to do anything he could to help me along, adding wistfully that he had long wanted

*Waterfalls cascaded down White Oak Canyon, along a side trail to Old Rag
Mountain, the most spectacular peak in the Central Appalachians.*

to try the trip himself. This is typical of the men who live and work in the parks. The ones I have known love the wilderness and the creatures that roam there. To them, cutting a tree is almost like killing an animal and neither should be done without good reason. Their busiest time is during the tourist season so they get no chance to tour themselves or take long hiking trips.

Eastward from Skyland is Old Rag Mountain, separated from the main ridge by a deep and narrow gorge. It is the most spectacular peak in the Central Appalachians, resembling on a smaller scale the Goat Rocks of the Cascades in Washington state. Old Rag is reached by a side trail down White Oak Canyon, passing scenic waterfalls before crossing the Old Rag Valley and traversing the shattered rimrock. This Mecca of hikers attracts many thousands of people every year, just as Katahdin does. The first of the "Byrd's Nest" shelters, financed and designed by former Senator Harry F. Byrd, Sr., is on Old Rag.

North of Skyland is an area of Blackstone Cliffs, described in Park literature as rock strata turned on end by some great upheaval in the past. They consist of huge boulders, like stone walls without mortar. One had fallen directly on the Trail. A Ranger I met later said he would notify officials so it would be removed. Geologically, the Blue Ridge in Virginia is mainly quartzite rock, obviously upthrust through limestone areas of the central valley and Atlantic coastal plain. The ridge rocks are generally volcanic in nature, with many colors and kinds of minerals displayed. The valley limestone and shale areas indicate the area was once under water. The shales contain many fossils.

By early evening the Lone Expedition came to Marys Rock, a great boulder pile overlooking Thornton Gap. The rock was named for his wife by Francis Thornton, who claimed the surrounding area and built a house in 1733. A toll road was built through the gap about 1800 to provide a route for farmers in the Shenandoah Valley to haul crops eastward to market. The inn in the gap had just closed but an employee got me some candy bars, the only food items available. He said some people had parked there and gone back to the shelter at Pass Mountain to stay overnight. Preferring a lone camp, I passed the side trail and slept at trailside. Starting early, for reasons of hunger, I came to Elkwallow, but the lodge had not yet opened.

Shenandoah National Park is an area returned to wilderness after being occupied by farmers for many years. Cattle raising was also common. Thousands of mountaineers lived there before the Park was established but life was hard. They moved to resettlement homesteads nearby or relocated elsewhere. The idea for the Park was promoted by Harold Allen, an early member of the Potomac Appalachian Trail Club, in a brochure printed and distributed by George H. Judd, a Washington publisher, in 1924. The plan was endorsed by the Pollack family, which had established the resort at

Skyland thirty years before. Tentative authorization came in 1926. The Potomac Appalachian Trail Club was organized to establish the A.T. along the crest of the Blue Ridge in Virginia, including the area that became the Park, and to foster appreciation and use of the Park. The Skyline Drive later disrupted the original route so much that it was replaced by new trail built by the CCC.

At Hogback Overlook I paused to photograph Massanutten Mountain in the valley westward, the picture including five of seven consecutive bends in the Shenandoah River. The name Massanutten supposedly derived from a cynical old man declaring they looked to him like "a big ol' mass o' nuthin'."

By midafternoon I was out of the Park and came in early evening to Route 522, where canned foods and bread were available at an inn. Then began a hectic quest for Mosby Shelter by flashlight, through an apple orchard and a section of recently logged timber. That little old leanto looked mighty welcome when finally found. Supper consisted of condensed vegetable soup, eight-serving size, a large can of peaches, and most of a loaf of bread. The famine was over, at least for a while.

Wood ticks were becoming a problem as I hiked through crisp, cool weather, along dirt roads mostly, to Linden, where a store down the road from the Trail crossing provided the usual staples. A thunderstorm was threatening again by the time I came to Ashby Shelter. I decided to stop early, since my boots and clothing needed repairs. Only one thing marred my stay after the storm bypassed down a valley. A phoebe had built its nest in the shelter and she fluttered away, calling anxiously, every time I entered. She must have come in after I was asleep because she flew out again when I moved in the morning. Before cooking breakfast I moved all gear outside so she wouldn't be disturbed again. Phoebes, like barn swallows, like to nest under the roof of a partially open building.

The shelter in Ashby Gap was only a few minutes' walk from the highway crossing. Two hikers had stayed in a tourist cabin there and were about to head south on the Trail. They were Charles Woodbury, a Class D (Individual) member of the Appalachian Trail Conference, who worked at the New York Public Library, and Mark Howard, a member of the Adirondack Mountain Club, who worked for the *New York Times.* They planned to spend a week on the Trail. North from the gap the Trail crossed a fence on a regular stile, far different from those hectic crossings in the Brier and Barbwire country. My noon stopping place was Three Springs Shelter. The sign said the springs were 75 yards away. Someone had added a zero. The distance paced off to about 230 yards. The one spring was so large that water might have been dipped by the barrel.

North from Snickers Gap the Trail followed the state line between Virginia and West Virginia. The most unusual spot along this section is the Devils Racecourse, on a side trail a quarter mile to the west. It is a long gently sloping rock area, like a ravine filled level, with a brook so far beneath that you hear it but never see it. Early evening brought me to Wilsons Gap Leanto, built of stone and with an inside fireplace. I should have stopped but hastened on, thinking of the rendezvous. Mileage was marked on rocks and I timed myself, covering four miles in fifty-five minutes, which is practically running. At dark I stopped and slept at trailside, a mile or two short of Keys Gap. The weather had been hazy and still was when the Lone Expedition arrived at Split Rock, overlooking Harpers Ferry and the juncture of the Shenandoah River into the Potomac. The three states of Maryland, Virginia, and West Virginia meet at this historic point.

Harpers Ferry was a focal point before and during the Civil War. John Brown, with only twenty men, captured the town and some of its citizens in 1859 as part of a planned campaign to end slavery. Two days later he and his band were killed or captured by a detachment of troops commanded by Robert E. Lee, then a Colonel, with Lieutenant J.E.B. Stuart second in command. During the war a few years later the town changed hands several times, and the railroad bridge was destroyed and rebuilt repeatedly. Harpers Ferry is now maintained as a National Historical Park by the National Park Service. The headquarters of the Appalachian Trail Conference, formerly located in Washington, D.C., is now in Harpers Ferry, near the Trail route.

The view from Split Rock shows the Potomac northwestward between West Virginia and Maryland and eastward through the gorge toward Washington. At one time a ferry crossing was necessary but a new bridge had just been completed and the Trail relocated over it, coming down from Split Rock over a steep trailway. That long, long haul over the Blue Ridge Mountains in Virginia had finally ended, and the Lone Expedition was now within striking distance of the halfway point. No one had ever come this far before. One effort before the war had ended just short of here. Captain Avery and several others had hiked all the Trail but not in one trip. That was the challenge remaining.

7

South Mountain Stroll

Out on the blue horizon
Under an ariel sky,
With aspect always sylvan
The days go strolling by.

NORTH OF THE BRIDGE the Trail looped down to the towpath of the Chesapeake and Ohio Canal, long since abandoned. The idea for a canal originated with George Washington before he became President, to provide a transportation route to the west. The towpath is now a National Historical Park. The A.T. follows it for about three miles until turning up Weverton Cliffs to the crest of South Mountain. This extension of the Blue Ridge is not high in comparison with other parts of the Appalachian Range but stands well above the adjacent countryside. Ledges like those in the Shenandoah extend for miles, with sheer precipices. At the top of Weverton Cliffs are traces of fortifications made by Union soldiers. This vantage point is a favorite with picnickers hardy enough to make the climb.

Farther north is Crampton Gap, a key position when General Lee tried to cross South Mountain to outflank and threaten Washington. In the gap is a gigantic archway memorial to War Correspondents, erected by George Alfred Townsend. Nearby are the ruins of Gathland, his mansion home. Clashes in this vicinity culminated in the Battle of Antietam. Plaques in Crampton Gap detail the various maneuvers in this hectic phase of the Civil War.

The Expedition came to Rocky Run Leanto about sunset, as the singing of robins and thrushes joined the purl of the nearby stream. Later a whip-poor-will was the vocalist. Could such a place be anything but restful? Then came Turners Gap and the original Washington Monument, erected on the mountaintop by the people of Boonsboro. This area is a State Park, complete with picnic tables, fireplaces, and comfort stations. The stone memorial, restored by the CCC, has a spiral stairway and an observation deck on top.

At trailside a few miles north was a sign painted on a boulder, "Annapolis Rock, 0.2 miles." It was a cliff with enormous boulders hanging on almost nothing, seeming to defy gravity. Black Rock and

Still visible from the A.T. in Crampton Gap, Md., is the War Correspondents Memorial Arch. The area is between Harpers Ferry, W.Va., and Sharpsburg, Md., the site of Antietam battlefield.

Raven Rock are similar places. Wolfe Leanto, near Smithsburg Road, was reached about an hour before sunset. Supplies were low as I headed for town, returning with only twenty-seven cents in my pocket but with enough food to last until the rendezvous with my father at Mont Alto. My supper was beef soup and bannock, mostly flour instead of cornmeal, baked in the frypan. A dog at a nearby farm howled at intervals all night.

Maryland also has a Devils Racecourse along the Trail, but it is larger and has a shelter nearby. The water source for the leanto is a pit dug down to the underground stream. From this point a trail leads to Catoctin Recreational Area. The weather was fine as I moved along, approaching the Mason Dixon Line, that historic but invisible line drawn to settle a dispute that brought on a war without battles between Maryland and Pennsylvania. The only indication of the line is a marker every mile. However, it symbolizes "North" and "South." Soon I was on familiar ground, the site of the Pen Mar Park,

The A.T. passes the nation's first Washington Monument, a stone structure erected by the people of Boonsboro, Md., on a nearby mountain in Turners Gap.

a resort that flourished years ago. After almost two months of foot-rambling in Dixie I was back in my native state.

At a refreshment stand near the line that twenty-seven cents down to the last copper, was squandered on soda and cookies, to celebrate and more or less as a lunch. I had promised to notify various people when reaching this point so mailed several cards before moving along to Mackie Run Leanto and stopping for the night. Fog rolled in before morning and logging had disrupted the Trail on the way to Antietam Leanto, where I talked with a fisherman before passing through Old Forge Campground and climbing to Chimney Rocks. The view from there was nullified by the fog. A mile or so beyond, a group of Boy Scouts approached. It was Troop No. 475, from Baltimore, led by Scoutmaster Roland T. Karchner, newly organized and on their first long hike—from Route 30 at Caledonia to Route 40 in Maryland. A thunderstorm was brewing so they hurried off, in hopes of reaching shelter.

The storm broke, with lashing winds and heavy rain, as I reached Snowy Mountain Tower and ducked under the porch of the Ranger's cabin. This was to be the rendezvous but no one was there, and no wonder. The weather was really atrocious. The storm abated an hour or so later and I went on down the Trail. My father was waiting at the first road crossing. He stared as though he couldn't believe his eyes. His middle son, roaming the mountains on foot, had actually turned up, alive and well!

The Forestry School of Pennsylvania State University is located near Snowy Mountain. The school originated in a cabin known as the Hermitage, the site of a cabin now maintained by the Potomac Appalachian Trail Club as a Trail cabin. Experimental plots of various trees and plants are maintained in the area between Snowy Mountain and Caledonia State Park. The oldest planting is a stand of white pines along Route 30 west of the Trail crossing. These trees, planted under the direction of Gifford Pinchot as one of the first sylviculture experiments in the United States, are now mature enough to cut for saw timber.

Before World War I, a magnificent stand of short leaf pines stood on the property of Benjamin George near Mont Alto. This was the northernmost range of the species. Average height was a hundred feet, without branches the first sixty feet, and diameters were two and a half to three feet. When asked about cutting them Mr. George always replied, "So long as my eyes remain open those glorious trees will stand." After his death in 1914, cutting of the trees began, using war need as the excuse. None of them remains today.

At the time of my trip my sister Ann was working at Mont Alto Sanatorium. She had attempted to meet me at the tower but was turned back by the violent storm. My Dad and I now went there to talk with her. It was decided I would return home to check over literature received from the Conference and to look at color slides returned from processing, to stay overnight at home because of the distance—about a hundred miles—and be brought back in the morning. This was the only night spent off the trailway. My youngest brother, John, brought me back and Sister Ann was waiting at Snowy Mountain with a picnic lunch.

Resuming the trek, I came to Caledonia Park, where crowds of people were everywhere, this being Sunday. At the crossing of Route 30 is the Thaddeus Stevens Blacksmith Shop. This building was captured and the nearby forge was destroyed when Confederate forces under General Lee passed on their way to the Battle of Gettysburg, returning the same way afterward.

About five miles east of the Trail crossing, at the headwaters of Conewago Creek, is White Squaw Mission. A young girl, Mary Jemison, was captured by Iroquois in Conestoga Valley, beyond the Susquehanna River, and brought up Conewago Valley, en route to their territory in western New York State, just north of Kinzua in

Enroute to Gettysburg, Pa., Confederate troops captured the Thaddeus Stevens Blacksmith Shop in what is now Caledonia State Park.

Pennsylvania. She later married a Seneca chief, and some of her descendants still live there. One of them, Abner Jemison, has shown me documentary proof of his lineage. A statue of Mary Jemison stands near the Old Mission and St. Ignatius Church, in Buchanan Valley.

Beyond the Blacksmith Shop in Caledonia Park is a large recreational area, and hundreds of people were picnicking or playing games as I passed through to Quarry Gap Leantos. Woodie Baughman, a lifelong friend, had decided to hike along a few days and joined me there. The weather was fine as we started off the next morning. Soon we were seeing the ant hills that are so numerous on South Mountain. Sometimes they are in groups, like villages, and some are five or six feet across and at least two feet tall. Naturalists say an ant hill is like a city in itself, with an organized society in which individuals perform certain tasks. They will react very promptly if the ant hill is disturbed. Their bite is very big for so small a creature and they do not come alone. An ant hill looks like a good place for a weary hiker to sit and rest, but surely isn't.

North of Caledonia is an area known as Big Flat, where some parts were burned over so completely that only scrub oak grows. Woodie and I arrived at Birch Run Leantos as three boys were preparing to leave. They were from Baltimore and had happened upon the shelter by chance. They spoke in awed voices of a bird that came close at night, its eyes glowing red in the firelight, and making a fearful noise. I imitated a whip-poor-will and they nodded excitedly. Ah, salad days! How I hated to tell them it wasn't a great horned owl.

Farther along Woodie and I passed Tumbling Run. The name is totally suitable. This stream drops from trailside on a steep slope in a crevice canyon, with many pools and fractured waterfalls. The place remains cool on a hot summer day.

On this same mountain ridge is a small tarn, its waters coming and going underground, inhabited by different species of frogs at different seasons, each so numerous that their voices create a continuous deafening sound. Also on this mountain are aftergrowths of the chestnut trees that once thrived here, large enough to produce chestnuts. Unfortunately, the shoots die after reaching a certain size and are replaced by others from the same stumps. The chestnut was once considered to be the most versatile and most valuable tree in Central Appalachia, before it was wiped out by an Oriental blight. Because of the persistent aftergrowth there is some hope that the species will someday re-establish itself.

Copperhead snakes are found along this section also. In fact my younger brother Evan and I killed a three-foot specimen when hiking there back in the thirties, when still in our middle teens. Woodie and I didn't see any but did come upon a milk snake, which looks very similar but is entirely harmless. After that Woodie said he was perfectly willing to walk second at all times. Actually, the danger of snakebite is almost nil on the Appalachian Trail. The greatest danger is crossing a busy highway, especially a four lane.

When hiking it is best to wear full length pants. If a snake does strike it is likely to catch the cloth instead of your leg. Bare legs are also an invitation to various insects,which are the bane of woods travelers. Poison ivy and sunburn are some of the other reasons for long pants.

At Toms Run Leanto the Trail branched, one loop traversing Sunset Rock and rejoining the main Trail at Pine Grove Cabin. As we approached I told Woodie of the time Evan and I came there and decided to pitch our tent in back. We had almost finished when a car came up the approach road, the people dashed up, unlocked the door, flung open the back windows, and there we were. No one could have decamped faster than we did. Just beyond the cabin are the ruins of Pine Grove Furnace. Some of the finest Franklin stoves ever made were produced there. The furnace was built in 1760 and was used to make weapons for the Continental Army, continuing in operation nearly a hundred and fifty years. The ore came from the pits farther down the valley that are now Fuller and Laurel Lakes, in Pine Grove Furnace State Park.

Woodie and I stopped at the store, located in a large stone building near the Ranger's headquarters. People lounging about stared but said nothing. As we were coming out a small boy ventured to ask where we were heading. When I mentioned Maine everyone suddenly crowded around. One of them was Duncan Harkin, a member of the Potomac Appalachian Trail Club.

Some parts of Big Flat, an area north of Caledonia State Park, had been burned over so completely that only scrub oak flourished.

We stopped at Whitestone Spring, just beyond Fuller Lake, and camped on a nearby "charcoal flat." These are seen in the vicinity of all the old furnaces and were the hearths used to burn the charcoal necessary in the iron-making process. Because of the threat of a storm we put up a poncho shelter but the storm never came over Holly Mountain. In the morning we passed the side trail to Pole Steeple, a quartzite outcrop overlooking Laurel Lake as though from an airplane. Across the valley is Holly Mountain, where I first caught "Mountain Fever." It was there, one night in October, that I first opened up a mountain spring and slept out under the moon and stars.

At Tagg Run, one of my old and favorite haunts, Woodie and I left our packs by the lower leanto while going upstream to the spring. My extra camera, which Woodie was using, was left with the packs. When we returned the Argus C3 was gone. Fishermen were in the area and a small village is nearby so we never did learn what became of it. Fortunately, my Retina was taken along. By evening we were at Whiskey Spring Leanto, named for a place that actually was about a mile away. The A.T. has since been relocated to pass the spring and the leanto is long gone. The name goes back to logging days when one of the timber cutters liked his whiskey cold and kept it hidden in a recess under a stone back of the spring.

In the morning Woodie and I crossed Long Mountain, climbing the firetower to survey the countryside. To the south, jutting from the Piedmont between Hanover and York, we saw the Pigeon Hills, named for the passenger pigeons that once nested there in great numbers. This beautiful bird, larger and more brightly colored than the mourning dove, was once considered the most numerous bird species on earth. A single flock would sometimes obscure the sun. They were exterminated by market hunters, the nestlings being considered a delicacy. Eventually, the birds still living, thousands of them, were too old to reproduce. When they died there was nothing.

Southeast of Long Mountain is another group of hills, with the Conewago Creek flowing through them in a deep and winding valley. Nestled among these hills is Gifford Pinchot State Park, surely one of the most beautiful in the country. Nearby is Roundtop, the highest and most impressive peak in York County. This was the first memorable mountain I ever climbed, with my oldest brother, Dan. We climbed the steep and rocky western side, and Dan almost had to drag me the last few hundred feet. The Gifford Pinchot Trail, from the A.T. to the Park, will soon be opened up across Roundtop and other peaks. Roundtop is now a popular skiing center.

At Long Mountain Woodie turned on a side trail toward Dillsburg, to catch a bus home. He didn't say so but his feet must have been hurting. The Trail turned through Dark Hollow, then up a steep pitch to Center Point Knob. This little peak, near the northern end of South Mountain, was calculated to be the original halfway point and was marked with a bronze plaque. Many changes have come since and the actual center will not be known until all the trailway is permanent. I paused at Center Point Knob to rest and to consider the future. So far my goal had been to reach Pennsylvania.

About two miles north of the knob is Boiling Springs, said to be the third largest spring in the world, with a flow of about a million gallons a day. The flow never changes and the temperature is always 51 degrees, regardless of season or weather. The water is almost pure, chemically, though it surfaces in a limestone valley, and the source is unknown. Hundreds of years ago this was a favorite Indian campground. Now it is the picturesque village of Boiling Springs. The Indian School at Carlisle, a few miles to the north, was made famous by Jim Thorpe, the greatest natural athlete this country has ever produced. He excelled in any sport the first time he tried it. Center Point Knob, and nearby areas, are still known to old timers as "Indian Peg," where local tribes held their councils.

South Mountain ends abruptly about two miles east of Center Point, near Dillsburg. This is the northernmost limit of the Blue Ridge, which is interrupted only by water gaps all the way to Georgia and Alabama. The general upthrust does continue east of the Susquehanna as a broken series of low ridges and pinnacles to the

Center Point Knob provided an appropriate spot for a picture at the original halfway point of the A.T. The bronze plaque had already been stolen from the monument.

Delaware River. The Appalachian Trail, of necessity, turns north and crosses the Great Valley to the Alleghenies.

There was no temptation now to head for home, though it was only twenty miles away. It had been a long and rugged hike but the beginning of June is not a proper time to stop walking with Spring. I had long since promised myself to keep going as long as nothing critical happened. Now the prospects were good for venturing to the highlands of New England and the end of the endless Trail. The Long Cruise would continue.

The former route through Pennsylvania's Cumberland Valley included the crossing of Yellow Breeches Creek at Brandtsville. The Trail continued on secondary roads, past occasional villages and many old stone and brick farm buildings.

8

Rock Ridge and Canopy Tree

With the touch of the mountainy breeze
Gently swaying the canopy trees
To a restless refrain,
On the rock ridge that pierces the sky
And in deeps where the brook voices cry
Shall we venture again?

LAUREL WAS BLOOMING at trailside, its fragrance on the breeze, as
the Lone Expedition started along White Rocks Ridge, now part of
the main Trail but then an alternate route. It is very scenic, much like
the timberline of New England, in miniature. The view from the
highest boulders shows Cumberland Valley farmlands and the long
high crest of Blue Mountain to the north. The Trail crossed Yellow
Breeches Creek at Brandtsville about three miles downstream from
Boiling Springs and headed across the valley on secondary roads,
passing occasional villages and many farms. These farms are very
distinctive, in the Pennsylvania tradition, with a large house, generally of stone or brick, a barn several times larger, usually facing
southeast, away from the wind and facing the morning sun, along
with other buildings such as a summerhouse, smokehouse, spring-
house, and sometimes an outhouse.

The Trail crossed Route 11, in the center of the valley at Silver
Springs, at an old tavern, believed to be the first stone building west
of the Susquehanna in Cumberland County. Route 11, coming from
Harrisburg, follows the approximate route of the "Great Warpath,"
which extended through the central valley to Cherokee territory in
the South. In the Susquehanna Valley it touched the Iroquois, or Six
Nations, to the northwest and the Lenni-Lenape Confederation to
the southeast. These were the three great Indian Nations east of the
Mississippi, similar but separate. The histories of the Iroquois and
Lenni-Lenape were best recorded by John Heckewelder in his book,
*History, Manners, and Customs of the Indian Nations Who Once Inhabited
Pennsylvania and Neighboring States.* For many years he was a mission-
ary and intermediary.

The Iroquois controlled the region from the Great Lakes into the valleys of the Allegheny, St. Lawrence, and upper Susquehanna Rivers, with the Seneca as the leading tribe. The Lenni-Lenape extended in a loose confederation from Maine to Virginia, with the Delaware as the central and largest tribe. The conflicts between these Indian nations and the settlers, and each other, were recorded in detail by Heckewelder, as well as the Indian governments, which were very democratic. He wrote that he sometimes was ashamed of being a white man.

In 1948 the Trail crossed the Conodoguinet Creek near Silver Springs. The stream winds through Cumberland Valley, a beeline distance of about fifty miles but at least five times that far along its banks, emptying into the Susquehanna north of Harrisburg. Conodoguinet is as wide as many a river in other parts of the country. Afternoon shadows were slanting across the smooth, reflective surface as I passed, creating a scene of picturesque beauty.

In one village I heard one woman say in a loud whisper, "I wonder where that guy's going." The other answered, "He's on the Appalachian Trail. It turns right there." Farther on a group of horseback riders came along, the shod hooves clattering on the road surface. A man hunting asparagus along a fencerow insisted on giving me what he had gathered. Near Blue Mountain a group of teenagers in front of a house stared humorously. Climbing the winding road toward Lambs Gap in the twilight I came to the Trail turnoff on the crest and stopped. That night I heard, in the stillness, a remarkable and ominous sound, millions of inch worms munching tree foliage overhead.

Along the ridge in the morning a large blacksnake refused to straighten from tight coils so it could be photographed. In southern Virginia one just as large kept straight as a stick and refused to coil. Several more miles of level trailway, typical of Blue Mountain, brought me to Overview, above the Susquehanna—the wide and shallow river. To the south sprawled Harrisburg, State Capital of Pennsylvania, and once considered for the national capital. To the north stretched Enola Railroad Yard, one of the largest in the world. Spanning the river in the gap was the famous stone arch railroad bridge, one of the longest in the world. This scene has been described by writers as one of the most picturesque scenes anywhere. The Trail descended steeply to the highway by the river, where a sign directed hikers to cross at the highway bridge at Harrisburg, several miles downstream. The railroad bridge was considered too dangerous.

I wanted to visit the city anyway. First stop was a shoe repair shop on Fifth Street, where an extra layer of sole was added before half soles and heels. These repairs put the Birdshooters in good shape again, and they lasted the rest of the way. True moccasin construction, with leather all the way under the foot is by far the strongest construction. These boots were elk hide, one of the best leathers to withstand frequent wetting and drying. I doubt that it is available now. Next on the list was a pair of Mountain Cloth pants and some socks. Along Front Street some hitch-hiking college students gave me the usual "look-at-the-character" stare.

During the French and Indian War a series of forts was built along Blue Mountain, under the direction of Benjamin Franklin, a man who seemed capable of almost any task. Fort Hunter was the one by the Susquehanna, in Dauphin Gap. A trading post already was in operation there and this was a focal point of travel and trade. Later it was an important link in the canal system that branched west along the Juniata. Dan Powers, one of my forebears who lived a few miles to the north in Perry County, was a canal boat captain and later piloted some of the gigantic white pine rafts that were floated down the Susquehanna.

The Appalachian Trail resumed near Fort Hunter, slanting up to the high point on the headland where a memorial honored Bishop James Darlington, originator of Darlington Trail along Blue Mountain. Moving along the ridge crest, I came in the twilight to Pletz Pass and followed the blue-blazed side trail down to the spring to stay overnight. Next day the Trail crossed Linglestown Rocks, known for a rank growth of poison ivy, to Heckerts Gap, where a jeep load of boys whizzed by. An hour later the Trail descended into Manada Gap where the Horse-shoe Trail branched off toward Valley Forge.

Marking faded and the Trail was overgrown beyond the gap. I struggled on, not knowing that this was part of the Indiantown Military Reservation, where the Trail had been closed because of proximity to an artillery range. At Indiantown Gap I came down a rock slide to the road and stopped to rest. A jeep came along and the driver, though dressed in fishing togs, including waist-high waiders, still had the look of an army officer. He thought the Trail followed the road past Moonshine Church to Swatara Gap, where the ridgetop trail resumed. He assured me there really was such a church.

After going that far—the church was there all right, with the name painted over the door—I found no signs of the Trail, decided the man was wrong, returned to bushwhacking along the ridge, and finally came to the road in Swatara Gap the next day, after sleeping under a hemlock high on the ridge. That was one of my roughest days, and no wonder! The section had really been closed since the beginning of the war. Years later I took a leading role in relocating the Trail from Swatara Gap over Second Mountain to St. Anthonys Wilderness on Stony Mountain, across Clarks Valley to Peters Mountain, across the Susquehanna at Clarks Ferry Bridge, over Cove Mountain, south to Deans Gap on Blue Mountain, and then

The shelter was called Applebee Cabin, the spring was Ludwig's Brun. Nearby was "Pilger Ruh," a resting spot for missionaries commemorated by members of the Blue Mountain Eagle Climbing Club.

across the Cumberland Valley on Ironstone Ridge. Except for Cumberland Valley, this route includes some of the finest trailway in the Central Appalachians.

A storm was approaching as I stood in Swatara Gap, wondering what to do. Supplies were very low and I ought to go out to Lickdale. Then I noticed an old man beckoning from the porch of a nearby house and hurried there just as heavy rain commenced. The man tried to greet me in broken English, then reverted to Pennsylvania Dutch, which I understand to some extent but cannot speak. He understood English so that's how we tried to communicate. He tried to tell some stories about the area in dialect but spoke so fast the details never did get straightened out.

When the rain stopped I left the pack on his porch and headed for town. A man in a Model A Ford took me down. When I came out of the store the same Ford was coming in the opposite direction. The timing was perfect. While riding along we discussed the car, which he had driven at least fifty miles per day, six days a week, for more than ten years, after buying the car secondhand. The old Lizzy was working fine as we buzzed on up the mountain. We agreed its durability was incredible.

Reclaiming my pack from my "deutschische" friend and saying "leb wohl," I crossed Swatara Creek, stopped to cook dinner at a spring, and was out on the ridge again when the ground seemed to explode under my feet. It was just another grouse hen and her chicks, all trying to take off at once. The fledglings had probably never flown before, landing clumsily on bushes and small trees while Mama tried to draw me away.

Applebee Cabin was the first shelter along the Trail since Whiskey Spring, and is located at Pilger Ruh, meaning Pilgrim's Rest, a spot named by Conrad Weiser and Count Nikolaus Ludwig von Zinzendorf, Moravian missionaries who stopped there while on their way to visit Indians in Wyoming Valley. The nearby spring is called Ludwig's Brun. A stone memorial was placed there by the Blue Mountain Eagle Climbing Club, which was formed by a hundred businessmen of Reading about 1920 and had built the original trailway between the Lehigh and Susquehanna Rivers. Danny Hoch was longtime president of the club.

About two miles beyond Pilger Ruh a sign at trailside said "Showers Five Hundred Steps," with a side trail branching to the right. This was puzzling at the time but is perfectly logical. Lloyd Showers, a local resident and a member of Blue Mountain Eagle Climbing Club, had shifted boulders on a rock slide to form a rough stairway down the mountain, to the Bethel-Pinegrove Road. People come from far and near to see this place. Farther along was Hertlein Cabin, in a well-watered cove. Camp gear was scattered around and voices from downstream led me to a pool where three young men were swimming. They offered to make room in the shelter, but I preferred sleeping in the woods in good weather. In the morning they helped clean up the mess left by previous occupants and even helped lay a stone walk across a swampy spot to the fireplace. They left in the direction of Showers Steps, while I cruised eastward, soon coming to a long, straight stretch of forest road. Along it was Pine Spring, so cold my teeth ached after a few swallows. Crushed stone had recently been spread on the road, each load colored differently. The Little Black Notebook says the stone "might have been taken from a petrified rainbow." The Trail led on.

From a high point overlooking the Schuylkill River, I looked down on Port Clinton. The birthplace of Daniel Boone is a few miles south of the town. As a boy he hunted and fished this area and in one instance he ventured through the gap into the far valley and stayed so long his family and friends went searching for him, finally locating him by spotting smoke coming out of a thicket. His family moved south when he was about fifteen. He visited the homestead twice during the 1780s. It is now maintained by the government as a historic site.

The post office in Port Clinton was closed so I camped beyond town on a charcoal flat, intending to return in the morning. Late at night a violent gust of wind and rain swirled through the forest and was gone as suddenly as it came. This reminded me of Zane Grey's description of Louis Wetzel, the border fighter, who made such a

A long straight stretch of forest road west of Port Clinton, Pa. Its many colors made it appear as if the crushed stone had come from "a petrified rainbow."

sound when attacking an Indian camp in dead of night. They called him Deathwind. The home of Zane Grey was along the Delaware River, not far from the Appalachian Trail.

In the morning I bought supplies and mailed film to be processed. Foggy rain moved in as I came to Windsor Furnace and the side trail to Pulpit Rock Pinnacle. In better weather the view from there is panoramic across the "Dutch" country of southeastern Pennsylvania. The Trail turns north across the valley at Eckville. Suddenly a violent thundergust roared out of the westward valley and I climbed the far far mountain in sloshy boots, soggy poncho, and drippy rainhat. I even stopped once to wring out my socks. At the summit was Dan's Pulpit, named for Congressman Hoch, who first introduced the "Trail Bill." Danny was one of the first of the Trail People I met after the Long Cruise.

A side trail in this vicinity leads to Hawk Mountain Sanctuary. Rock ledges on the crest cause an updraft and migrating hawks and eagles swoop low to ride the wind. Years ago men came with guns to shoot the birds, slaughtering them by the thousands. Laws were passed but probably came too late. Like the mighty condor, almost extinct because of "prestige" killing, the hawks and the eagles are dwindling year by year.

Beyond Dan's Pulpit the real storm of the day arrived. The Little Black Notebook says, "It rained as fast as the air would let it fall, while I stumbled along the rocky trail, feet sloshing, water trickling down my neck, and telling myself I had to be crazy to start this ridgerunner marathon in the first place." That made the consensus practically unanimous. Rain still fell as I side-trailed to Allentown Shelter, and was surprised to find it occupied by three boys. They were celebrating the closing of the school year, but looked mighty sorry right then. They had lit a fire in the center of the shelter with the last of the firewood. Then came another surprise, arrival of Clarence Stein, father of one of the boys. He had become worried, for good reason. Mr. Stein and I then ventured out to the wet woods to gather wood, doing a good deed for the Boy Scouts. The roof leaked but morning finally came. They soon left for home but I remained, to reorganize and dry out a little.

The weather was beautiful now as I started off over brush-choked trail. Once a slight movement ahead stopped me short. It was a grass snake, green as the foliage around it, sunning itself on a huckleberry bush. It stayed long enough to be photographed. These beautiful little creatures are so well camouflaged and so shy that they are seldom seen. Then a strawberry patch yielded a hatful of fruit and I carried them along to Matz Valley Leanto and stopped there to bake bannock panbread in lieu of shortcake. At this shelter was a register supplied by "Sam and Flo," Class D Members of ATC. Months later they wrote that they were in the Nantahalas at the time of my passing through, heard of me from Warden Buchanan, but never managed to be at the right place to intercept me.

North of Allentown are many rock ledges. From one of these I turned the camera toward the city across the Lehigh Valley farmlands, then down to the never-never, the tops of trees hundreds of feet below. This gave me a strange feeling, as though I could step down and walk on the treetops, a dangerous flight of fancy. North of here are the anthracite coal fields, first discovered at Mauch Chunk about 1750. Anthracite is so hard it is sometimes used for souvenir carving.

Another storm threatened during the afternoon and I practically ran for several miles, looking for shelter, but the storm turned down a parallel valley and I stopped to camp on a charcoal flat by a spring, not far from Lehigh Gap. From there in the morning I side-trailed to Palmerton for supplies, then climbed the steep and rocky incline out of the gap. This definitely was not the place for a "ridin' critter." Various people have tried to use horses, mules, donkeys, and even motorcycles to traverse the Appalachian Trail, but "Shanks Mare" seems to be the only way. This was emphasized at one of the Sam and Flo registers, where a New Yorker had written, "What are these, the Appalachians or the Rockies? My feet feel like hamburgers."

Entirely different in tone was an entry by Ernest Greiser, of Easton: "Sun and wind and the sound of rain—Hunger and thirst and strife—God, to be on the Trail again—With a grip on the mane of life."

Wind Gap definitely deserves its name, according to a man I met there. He said that air currents are channeled by the terrain so that a wind blows on the calmest day. The four-lane highway is the southern gateway to the Pocono Resort region, known for its lakes and waterfalls. As usual I had to scurry across that highway to avoid the cars and trucks zooming over the crest. Speed limits are always too high at such places and seldom are enforced anyway.

East of Wind Gap was the nastiest predicament on the trek. Inch worms, larvae of the gypsy moth, were literally stripping the foliage from an entire forest of chestnut oak. The pesky things were everywhere, swinging on webs from every twig, crawling on the ground, up my pants legs, into my eyes and ears. They couldn't even be brushed off without squashing. It took me four long hours to get through the infested area. The plague of the gypsy moths is gradually spreading across the country in spite of spraying and other attempts at control.

The Trail became narrow and rocky for a few miles before coming to a rock ledge overlooking the Delaware River. Tammany Mountain loomed high on the New Jersey side. This peak, named for one of the Delaware chiefs who signed the treaty with William Penn, features a curving rock stratum. This helps to explain an Indian legend that the area to the north, toward the Poconos, had once been a large lake held by the mountain, which finally broke. They called this region the "Minisink," meaning "the water is gone." I slept on the ledge, in hopes of a sunrise picture over Tammany Mountain, but cloud conditions were hopelessly dull in the morning.

William Penn got along well with the Indians, sometimes staying with them for days. He enforced treaty boundaries and punished offenders. His heirs changed that. When negotiating a treaty to acquire the land as far as Blue Mountain, using the usual "Day's Walk," about twenty miles, as measurement, they hired a man named Marshall, who walked twice as far, despite Indian objections, and claimed the land far beyond Blue Mountain, into the Minisink. This is known historically as the "Walking Purchase," which helped bring on the French and Indian War.

Eventually the Delawares and the rest of the Lenni-Lenape were displaced entirely, being squeezed between the colonies and the Iroquois, the remnant fleeing westward beyond the Mississippi, where their ancestors had lived, according to tradition. A few individuals remained behind, regardless. The real "last of the Mohicans" died in his wickiup on Kittatinny Mountain, overlooking his beloved Minisink, retaining his Indian heritage.

My breakfast was cooked at a spring in a rhododendron thicket on the way down to the river. Just beyond was a small pavilion, where I stopped to take a picture. A tall old man came strolling up the path, wearing dark suit and white shirt, straight as a ramrod, and swinging a beautiful blackthorn cane. He said he had been coming to Delaware Water Gap for more than fifty years and still considered it his favorite resort. He spoke of many places, having traveled much of Europe and North and South America. My own travels in the Pacific during wartime interested him greatly. As we started down the path together he quoted Scripture, "Young men shall see visions, old men shall dream dreams," adding, "I come here to dream." When we came to the side path leading to his hotel he raised his hand and turned away with a softly spoken "Vaya con Dios," the old Spanish farewell.

The resort at Delaware Water Gap, with its waterfalls, its rhododendron gardens, and its scenic ledges, was a very popular place in past years. Chartered trains carried hundreds and even thousands of people on weekend excursions at speeds comparable to highway speeds of today. The difference in cost and fuel consumption, and the greater margin of safety, are easily imagined. In those days such scenic places as Watkins Glen, Pen Mar, and Delaware Water Gap were widely known and discussed.

At the road next to the river, a man sitting on a porch said the nearest bridge was about five miles down stream at Portland. He suggested I wade across, that the water would scarcely reach my knees. One glance at that wide expanse convinced me otherwise. Somewhere out there was a channel. Needing color film, which wasn't available in the local store, I caught a bus to Stroudsburg. On the way back I hitched a ride with a war veteran named Shillereff. He told of being one of the only seven men who survived when his Ranger Battalion was ambushed and massacred by German tanks in Italy. The seven were away on patrol at the time. He took me right on through to Portland, where the bridge was the type often pictured on calendars. It was a wooden covered bridge, of the style seen in New England and Pennsylvania, with massive hand-hewn timbers, arched span supports, and protective roof and siding. Nailed to one of the corner posts was a metal A.T. marker. My battered old boots thudded softly on the heavy planking as I crossed to the Garden State of New Jersey.

A stiff climb on the curving rock ledge of Tammany Mountain provided a late afternoon view of the Delaware River, separating Pennsylvania and New Jersey. A highway bridge is there now.

9

Lakes and Jumbled Hills

Crystal Lakes on the crest of the range,
Chance meetings, both friendly and dire,
Stoney footing and weatherly change,
And the bane of forbidden fire.

MOST OF NEW JERSEY is coastal plain, with level or gently rolling farmlands or pine barrens, but the part next to the Delaware River is definitely mountainous. The Appalachian Trail follows Kittatinny Ridge, with the Delaware River Valley and the Poconos to the west. This region was unexpectedly wild and picturesque, with many whitetail deer and other wildlife. But this was more than thirty years ago. From Portland Bridge some patches of berries slowed me but I finally arrived at the base of Tammany Mountain, where a stiff climb on the curving rock ledge took me to the summit.

Far below lay the river, winding from the north through the Minisink, with the late afternoon sun lighting the surface, placid except for the V-shaped wake of a small power boat. Beyond lay the Pocono Mountains, once the beloved homeland of the Lenni-Lenape but now the vacation haunts of countless city dwellers. A four-lane bridge now spans the river in the gap, eliminating the detour to Portland, along with the pastoral view.

My camp that night was a few miles north and was one of those impromptu arrangements that turn out right. Rain was beginning to fall and in my haste to make a shelter before the ground got wet I slanted a pole in a tree fork and threw the poncho across, then tied two other poles to left and right from the peak, forming what really was half a wigwam. Actually the tree was not necessary, as the three poles formed a tripod when tied together. Once again I had reverted to Indian ways, and this became my standard shelter henceforth. The center opening was covered with my rainhat.

The snorting of deer awoke me in the morning. They had come very close before catching my scent. When I poked out my head they leaped away and vanished in the woods. The storm was over, the weather after-rain, cool and clear, with foliage glistening green, a fine time for hiking except for the drenching grass and brush. More deer moved ahead as I came to Sunfish Pond, the first natural lake on the A.T. going north. From here to Katahdin, lakes are the usual thing.

North from Sunfish Pond the Trail was often rough and rocky through scraggly brush, passing Sand Lake and Fairview Lake before coming to the shelter near Harding Lake. I would have stopped but the place was strewn from here to yonder with numerous bedrolls and other gear, while shrill voices from the direction of the lake and various unmentionables scattered about indicated that a group of girls was in residence. One hasty glance was enough to send me off, practically at a lope. Rain began later as I hurried over rocky terrain and finally was forced to stop and try to sleep while huddled under the poncho, no shelter, no supper, no nothin', except definitely misogynistic thoughts.

Rain still fell in the morning as I came to Brink Shelter but a clear-up wind began to blow and the rain stopped as I reached a point overlooking Culver Lake, then descended to a gap and a grocery store. Since a fire was forbidden in New Jersey I bought only things that needed no cooking. The next shelter was of stone but had no water supply. At least it was dry and I was able to get some much needed sleep. At Sunrise Mountain next day I met a family group at the stone pavilion. The day was Sunday and a road came near. One of the men insisted that at least five people had already hiked the entire Appalachian Trail, and he was very provoked when I disagreed. He couldn't seem to realize the difference between hiking the whole Trail in several hikes, requiring years, and hiking it all the way continuously. Actually, six people had hiked the Trail in a series of hikes. They were Myron Avery, Dr. George Outerbridge, Charles Hazelhurst, Mr. and Mrs. Martin Kilpatrick, and Orville Crowder.

At High Point State Park there were lots of picnic fireplaces but none was being used and they looked as though they seldom were. At each was a sign reminding that a permit from a Ranger for exact time and place was required. The signs did not indicate where or how you could find a Ranger. No through hiker could possibly meet such requirements. I rambled on, passing the villages of Unionville and Liberty Corners in New York State, then veering back into New Jersey, mostly on roads. Once a friendly dog about two-and-a-half feet high and twice as long tried to join the Expedition. He tagged along for several miles, despite attempts at friendly persuasion, before I resorted to sticks and stones to turn him back.

Dogs either love or hate a person carrying a pack. Hounds are usually the friendliest. Beware of German shepherds, chows, and similar breeds. Terriers are small but nasty. One came yapping at my heels along a blacktop road. Suddenly a chow dashed out from a house and made a leaping grab. I fended him off with my forearm but got a bloody gash. The owner heard the commotion, came around from behind the house, denied the dog had bitten me, and berated me for being on the public highway, and then threatened to call the police. I told him to go ahead, and save me the trouble. Meanwhile the dog crouched wolfishly at his side and he made no move to punish it. I concluded the dog was not rabid, just vicious, like its master, and bandaged the cut myself later.

Dark fell as I reached Wawayanda Mountain, where I slept under a giant hemlock tree, near a waterfall. South wind promised rain but not before morning. It came on schedule and my feet soon were soaked. While I rested on a bank later, wringing out my socks, a Labrador retriever came up and sat beside me, in a friendly fashion, until I rose to leave. At least nine out of ten dogs are friendly, even to a backpacker, but beware of the others. Later, along a woods road, a man came walking and I waited for him to catch up. He remarked about the Trail being relocated because of the nudist camp. This didn't really register until later. The Trail crossed overgrown fields and came out where some buildings and a pond were being built. It looked like another dude ranch—not unusual in New Jersey—but apparently wasn't. The people who were there looked at me strangely—probably imagining my appearance without clothes. Later on, I read an AP story about the camp. Still later, another story said the camp had failed because of a mosquito problem.

Turning northward, the Trail followed a ridge, overlooking Greenwood Lake to the east, in the direction of New York City, which would be visible on a clear day. The weather was beginning to clear as the Lone Expedition crossed into New York State and the Palisades Interstate Park. The Little Black Notebook says "Sure am glad to be out of New Jersey. That no-fire law has me on the verge of starvation, and pneumonia." At the north end of Greenwood Lake a trail branched down to a village of the same name. The delicatessen was run by an Irish lady, who was amazed that anyone actually —could have walked all the way from Georgia, on the mountains. Yet her eyes twinkled as though she were thinking, "Yes and you can be sure that such a one would be looking a wee bit Irish." This wouldn't be far-fetched. My mother was a Gallagher. The lady urged me to try a can of corned beef and cabbage, which actually was in stock. After all, why not? Has it not been estimated that more Irishers live in the New York area than in Erin itself?

New York State is stern about fire-building, but logically. The penalty for causing a fire is severe, including the cost of fighting the fire and the resulting damage. I repeat: Dangerous fires are those built away from water and left smouldering. "Drown your fire" is a must for woods travelers. And if you must smoke, be careful with discards. I have never smoked, and never will.

After a few more miles of cruising along, I stopped and slept under hemlock trees near a spring. The corned beef and cabbage was delicious. Next morning at Inspiration Point the vista was far and fine. The name itself inspired:

Jumbled green hills across a wide expanse
Of forestland where wild birds freely sing,
And teeming hordes of new grown foliage dance
Upon the blithesome zephyr breeze of Spring,
The warbling of a woodthrush far below,
A flicker calling in staccato tone,
The raucous croaking of a fledgling crow
Waft upward to this lofty ledge of stone.

These hills were much the same long years ago
When first the restless-hearted white man came,
When life was hard and blood was quick to flow
And those who followed trails were not so tame
As I and such as I who come and gaze
In reverie across the mountain maze.

Palisades Interstate Park is a woodland playground for millions, north of New York City and easily accessible. The first miles of trailway built deliberately for the A.T. were built there, under Park leadership, soon after Benton MacKaye suggested the project. The insignia universally associated with the Trail originated there.

The proprietor of a service station in the village of Arden, where I stopped to get a map, told of a man who woke up one morning at a shelter and found his bacon gone, even though he had hung it from a tree limb. The next night he hung out some more and stayed awake to watch, finally seeing a raccoon climb up and repeat the theft. So what happened at Fingerboard Mountain Leanto shouldn't have surprised me.

The shelter is built of stone, on top of a gigantic boulder, with a tin roof and a fireplace in each end wall. The water supply is far downhill, so I brought in an extra kettleful and set it on a ledge to be handy in the morning. My pack was slung overhead to discourage mice. The moon was crystal bright. About midnight the kettle rattled, waking me in time to see a ringed tail disappear around the corner. The second time the 'coon didn't bother to leave, just sat and blinked when I shined a light. Then the rascal discovered a box of spaghetti someone had left in the shelter, picked it up with forepaws and hopped out front in the moonlight, ripped open the box and began to chew noisily, got thirsty and drank from my kettle, and went back to the pasta again. My only regret was lack of flash equipment for the camera.

Next time it was dirt falling on my face that awoke me. The 'coon was now bold enough to try to reach my pack, which was directly above my head. This required some upside down gymnastics. I yelled and it scrambled away, but soon came back. Now I was ready with a long stick and whacked the pesky critter a few times. This time it stayed away but dawn soon came. I stared at the shelter roof for a moment wondering. Had I been dreaming? One glance out front was sufficient. There was the evidence, the chewed remains of a pound of spaghetti.

At Lake Tiorati Circle I stopped to register at the Rangers Station. The trailway beyond was plagued by mosquitoes and black flies, the latter so vicious I muffled my head in my sweater. The flimsy netting obtained in Virginia had long since disintegrated. At Letterrock Mountain another stone shelter had a fireplace in a stone center column. Beyond was a lookout showing Bear Mountain and the Weather Station on the summit. The ascent of Bear Mountain was up the steep face. Near the top, chiseled into solid rock, was this inscription: "Vogel State Park, Georgia, 1200 miles." The view south from Bear Mountain is over the Tappan Zee, where the Hudson River widens to four miles before narrowing again at the Palisades. This region was featured in the stories of Washington Irving, about the Dutch who first colonized New York.

North of Bear Mountain is the West Point Military Reservation. During the Revolution a colossal hand-forged chain was stretched across the river to prevent the British Fleet from going upstream. The chain was held up by enormous wooden floats, and stretched from Bear Mountain to Anthony's Nose on the opposite shore. This peak supposedly was named by Henry Hudson because of a resemblance to one of his crewmen. A museum and amusement park are operated by the State Park Commission and the American Museum of Natural History at Bear Mountain.

The crossing of the Hudson River was on the Bear Mountain Bridge, a massive structure similar to the Golden Gate Bridge at San Francisco. To my astonishment I was charged five cents to walk across, the only toll paid on the Long Cruise. It's a wonder they didn't charge me truck rates. This crossing, incidentally, is the lowest point on the Appalachian Trail, the river being practically at sea level. The Trail ascended St. Anthony's Nose, on steep and rocky footing. From topside the view of the Catskills to the northwest recalled the story of Rip Van Winkle. Was this the twentieth year, by any chance, when Henry Hudson and his crew of the Halfmoon return for their legendary carousal?

East from the river the Trail crossed level terrain, sometimes swampy and ideal for mosquitoes. To escape them I camped that night on an exposed spot above a large boulder and started a smudge fire, putting it to windward so the smoke would pass above my head. This helps and isn't too bothersome, as long as you keep your head down. Fine weather, sunny and breezy, encouraged rapid progress the following day, through a region of small lakes, bordered by masses of flowers. Then came Canopus Lake and a devious path to the leanto on the far side. This shelter stood on a mossy ledge and was neatly built, the logs being so uniform and so nicely notched that no chinking was necessary. Surprisingly, there was almost no vandal carving. On the back wall was a register, containing many comments on the spring. One said, "The water looks green but it tastes all right." I didn't need to sample it. Rain came and fell intermittently throughout the night, filling a kettle placed under the overhang, and stopping before daylight. This was the last shelter seen for several days.

From Canopus Lake the Trail passed through a region of summer homes, mostly on roads, and passed Taconic Parkway. Just beyond, nailed to a tree, was a hand-painted sign announcing a grocery store in the front room of a nearby house. The lady said she had started the enterprise because her neighbors complained of having no place to buy food in the community. Every item she stocked was judged on whether her own family approved it. Four or five Scotch-Irish offspring looked none the worse for their role as guinea pigs. In fact they looked real healthy and rambunctious. Farther along the day turned foggy as I came to a quiet glade, where a slight movement to the side alerted me to a whitetail doe and her fawn, moving slowly through the undergrowth. So like a slim young heifer browsing by—and closely followed by her spotted fawn. A stumble-step, a self rebuking sigh—and silently as wraiths the two were gone.

Then the Trail turned between some ramshackle, unpainted buildings. A puzzling quietude, almost abandonment, was there and yet I sensed a presence. Beyond the buildings the Trail became well worn, with a wire stretched alongside on poles. Then a little old man with a long stick was coming slowly toward me. His head was turned toward a robin singing somewhere in the mist. On his face was a rapt expression. He didn't seem to hear my greeting at first, then answered in a low voice, with a gentle smile and downcast eyes, and moved on by. Only then did I realized that the old man was blind and that someone had stretched the wire along the Trail for him to follow through the woods, by means of the staff.

At the village of Holmes, during the afternoon, I paused to perform a momentous duty. So far the Appalachian Trail Conference had received no communication from me, but the time had come. A conference was scheduled to begin within a few days at Fontana Village in North Carolina and a message of greeting was appropriate. Unless something drastic occurred the success of my trek was now assured and I ought to let my presence be known. On a folded sheet of paper I sketched a likeness of the Pinnacles of the Dan and put beneath:

The flowers bloom, the songbirds sing
And though it sun or rain
I walk the mountain tops with Spring
From Georgia north to Maine.

The fire "hissed and warbled almost a melody" as a light rain fell. The firelight, reflecting from the leaves overhead, created a niche in the solitude of Macedonia Brook State Park.

Inside was the date of departure from Oglethorpe and the expected date of arrival at Katahdin. Months later I was told by Jean Stephenson that the message was received in the mail at Fontana. Is it somewhere in ATC files?

Much of the Trail in eastern New York followed roads, passing the properties of such prominent individuals as Lowell Thomas, the famous traveler and news commentator, and Thomas Dewey, then a candidate for the Presidency. At Pawling I got involved in a discussion about the army and the late war, delaying me so much that daylight was fading as I hastened through Quaker Hill. Bad weather was closing in as I finally turned aside into a dense woods and spent an uncomfortable night in the rain. "Talkin' when you should have been walkin'," says I to myself.

The morning takeoff was "soon," but the weather improved as I passed through Webatuck and came to the Connecticut line at Schaghticoke Mountain. According to the register there, the place ought to be called Rattlesnake Heaven, or just the opposite, depending on the viewpoint. Entries indicated that forty or more of the noisesome reptiles had been killed or captured by hikers or snake hunters within a few years' time. The area now seemed clear of them but the advice was to avoid sitting down before looking. Another entry was by two girls who had evidently come from the other direction over rugged terrain. The entry said, "We hate the Appalachian Trail, so there." Perhaps they had even come over the Ledge Loop, which I was to see shortly.

At a fork in the Trail one sign said, "Notch Loop, for use in bad weather or with heavy loads." The other said "Ledge Loop, Strenuous—Dangerous in wet or icy weather." You can guess which one I chose. The ledges sometimes were no more than a foot wide but the real hazard was an overhang, scaled by means of a tire chain dangling from a tree root. The only way was by rappelling in reverse, hand over hand, with feet or knees against the cliff. The chain and the root withstood the strain, and so did I, just barely. In the far valley was a rocky knoll, with the topside boulders covered with painted names and initials. At the very top was a wooden cross in remembrance of a twenty-year-old man.

By early evening the Lone Expedition entered Macedonia Brook State Park and came uphill through the twilight to a nice leanto. This was the first shelter since Canopus Lake, a very welcome sight. Later, when the fire had burned low, a light rain began falling, pattering on the roof and pelting the fire so that it hissed and warbled almost a melody. The firelight reflected from leaves overhead, creating a niche in the solitude, like a room in the *Green Mansions,* immortalized by Hudson.

Curtains of the Sky

No mighty peaks, yet picturesque,
with unexpected hills,
A charming backyard wilderness
that adequately fills
Trail time with tinkling waterfalls
and tall cathedral pines,
White birch and broken boulder walls,
and honeysuckle vines.

COBBLE MOUNTAIN provides a far-reaching view across the Hudson Valley to the Catskills. These mountains, like the Poconos, were once a favorite dwelling place of the Indians, and were known to them as "Curtains of the Sky." After crossing Cobble Mountain the Trail descended steeply over ledges and rocks and followed the Housatonic River for several miles. Coming unexpectedly into one small clearing on the river bank I surprised a large bald eagle sitting on a rock in the river. It took wing instantly and soared away above the treetops. This was the only bald eagle definitely identified during the Long Cruise. Our national bird is a vanishing species, unable to live with civilization. The same might be said of the Mohicans, an Indian tribe immortalized by James Fenimore Cooper. Centuries ago they had a village along the Housatonic.

Near Cornwall Bridge a man stopped along the road to offer a ride. He had the appearance of a person equally at ease in a board of directors meeting or on a wilderness trip. When told of my trek he wistfully declared he would like to join me the rest of the way but couldn't. At the grocery store in the village the choice of food was typical of New England; I even got some Boston brown bread. Beyond town the Trail turned up a beautiful ravine under towering hemlocks, often along the brink of a miniature gorge where little waterfalls fell or cascaded over mossy rocks into clear deep pools. The canopy was so dense that only stray bits of pure sunlight got through. This was Dark Entry, one of the beauty spots along the Appalachian Trail.

Beyond was a plateau region of broken terrain, with giant boulders next to tiny grass plots and clumps of white birch, silver maple, and other colorful trees. Sometimes the Trail blazes were painted on black spots painted on white trees. Then the Trail turned on roads for a while before coming to Cathedral Pines. This grove of trees reminded me of the Smokies, many of them towering at least a hundred feet. One giant sits directly on top of a boulder, about six feet from the ground, and with roots reaching down on all sides.

About sundown I came along the edge of a game refuge and through abandoned farms to The Pinnacle on Clark's Hill, reaching the road on the top at twilight. Just then a voice startled me, coming from a young couple who were strolling and had thought I was someone they knew. This man had been on Katahdin, which he called "The greatest mountain in the world." One of his friends had reached the summit on skis, one of the few who ever had. He had intended trying to go all-the-way on the Appalachian Trail himself but had given up the idea. I suspected that the reason was with him right then. The young lady didn't seem interested in such things. Their car was parked nearby. I moved along and soon stopped to sleep under some pines. Soon after starting in the morning I came to a nice leanto and stopped for breakfast, then came to another an hour later.

Many white birches were at trailside as I went through an area of summer colonies, such as Yelping Hill and Music Mountain. Nearby is Dean Ravine, a favorite with artists from the camps, with waterfalls that rivaled those in Dark Entry. The Trail followed a brook to a road, then up a rocky ledge, and back to the road again before reaching Falls Village. This was typical of the route through Connecticut, a sort of backyard wilderness. Some more of this included one big black dog that came with hackles rising. Fortunately the owner was near and called it off. Then the road dwindled to a tote-road and a sign saying: "Remember Bar Harbor," and finally a lumber camp. Beyond was more broken terrain, with fissures as though from a subterranean collapse. Dark was near by now but the place was gloomy. I kept on until forced to stop at the best spot in a swampy area. It was one of those long, long nights.

More murky weather and overgrown trail greeted me in the morning. As a last resort I started singing to cheer myself up. If anyone had heard he surely would have thought a lunatic had escaped somewhere. At a road crossing near Salisbury, I turned aside to get supplies. Rainfall was heavier than ever as I stood under an awning in front of a store, mustering the courage to face the downpour. The proprietor of an adjoining barroom came out to scan the weather and remarked that the Louis-Walcott fight would probably be postponed. This didn't register for a moment. Prize fighting was not important just then. The rain didn't ease so I stuck my head through the poncho, put on the rainhat, and started off in the same dogged way a punchy fighter goes out for another round. Morale was at low ebb, lowest of the trek.

The rain kept on and so did I, coming through brush and grassland to a solitary house, beyond a barbwire fence. Where the Trail went I didn't know and scarcely cared. I flopped down and was crawling under the fence when a voice came from the doorway, telling me the gate was to my right. Being halfway, I kept on crawling. The man insisted I come into the house, despite my soggy condition. He and his wife began to feed me coffee and cookies. He had been in the Pacific too, in the Marines, and on some of the same islands as I. He knew a bit about hardship himself. My spirits began to rise. No one could have been more hospitable than they, or as understanding. They didn't even tell me I was crazy—to which I would have readily agreed.

My recollection of crossing Bear Mountain, highest peak in Connecticut, at 2335 feet, is vague, but I must have signed the register because people have written about it. Visibility was practically minus. Sages Ravine is said to be beautiful, but I didn't notice. Sometime, somewhere, I crossed into Massachusetts, home state of Benton MacKaye, and finally stopped for the night on a ledge behind some rocks. A poncho shelter and a drying and warming fire did help, and the rain stopped during the night.

At dawn the skies cleared completely and the clouds dropped into the valleys. Mt. Everett was close ahead, while Bear Mountain, with its stone monument on the summit, towered on the back Trail. Someone has said that if you don't like the weather in the Appalachians, just wait a while and it will change. This time it had taken pretty long. My clothing and gear were almost dry by the time I reached the tower on Everett. A young couple came up the Trail, said they had "cheated" by driving as close as they could. The good weather held during most of the way along the ridge, but lightning and thunder announced the approach of another storm as I scrambled down the end of the ridge near South Egremont and hugged the trunk of a dense limbed tree. The downpour lasted at least an hour, while a swarm of mosquitoes did their best to profit from the situation. As I started off, a station wagon with siren wailing came skidding and roaring from the rear. Surely there was a lightning fire somewhere, but the vehicle was parked by a house farther along. The driver probably was just having fun, or was in a hurry to get home.

Clouds were racing overhead as I came to a point where a sign indicated a valley crossing eastward. But marking in that direction was lacking and I finally knocked on a door to get directions. The door opened and a husky young man wearing Marine fatigues looked at me. When asked about the Trail he said that explained the white marks he had seen on posts and trees, that it followed the "Bow Wow Road," pointing to a sign at the intersection. Originally it was the "Pow Wow Road" because Indians once held councils there, but later residents thought that name was silly and changed it. As I was about to turn away he invited me to dinner, adding with a laugh, "that is if you don't mind hash." He and his wife were a handsome couple, dark haired and dark eyed. His name was Louis Mazarelle, and his family lived in Maine. They were timber men and he was a power saw operator for a lumber company based in Sheffield.

Hash actually was on the menu but garnished with onions and really very tasty. Before I left, Lou declared I needed more clothing and insisted on giving me an old combat shirt he said he would never need. It proved very useful farther north when cold weather set in. At the main road north of Sheffield I hid the pack and headed for town, but had trouble getting a ride and got there after the stores were closed. Getting back was just as bad and dark caught me as I stumbled on past a reservoir and finally stopped under some towering pines. Rain was resuming and necessity resulted in another of my unorthodox arrangements. Setting the pack on a thatch of pine needles, I laid the poncho with the neck opening over the top of the pack and covered the opening with my rainhat. Then I huddled underneath, next to the pack. In a pinch this is much better than no shelter at all.

Next day conditions became almost unbearable. The Trail followed an abandoned railroad bed across a plateau region where brooks had overflowed and were flowing down the Trail, forcing me to wade kneedeep in muddy water. Singing "River Stay 'Way From My Door" didn't influence the elements but did tickle my sense of humor. Near Great Barrington a friendly old man came along on a two-horse wagon, bound for his woodlot for a load of poles. He said that the area had once been prosperous farmlands and that some foundations of houses and barns could still be found. He didn't seem to mind the miserable weather.

Beyond town the Trail entered Beartown State Forest and passed several lakes. Water level at Benedict Pond was so high that the Trail was flooded. The sky cleared as I reached Tyringham and stopped at the general store to mail cards and get supplies. My bed that night was under hemlocks on a ridge, without rain. Morning weather was fair and I was making good time past Yocum Pond when two men came round a bend clearing trail. One was cutting limbs with a long-handled shears and throwing them aside, while the other was swinging a weeder. They were members of the Metawampe Club, outing club of the University of Massachusetts faculty. They told me that two others were ahead, one of them John Vondell, president of the New England Trail Conference, vice-president of the Green Mountain Club, president of the Metawampe Club, and member of the Board of Managers of the Appalachian Trail Conference. Yet he somehow managed to be a university professor, the only job that paid anything.

At noontime I stopped by a brook to cook in my usual fashion. First a spot was cleared of litter and duff. Dead twigs were gathered and laid to one side. A kettle of water was set on the other side and the pack was used for a back rest. Corncake was baking in the pan and soup was simmering in the kettle, when the other two men came busily down the Trail. The second stopped suddenly, looked over and said, "Aha, I thought I smelled a smudge." It was John Vondell, a key figure in the Trail project in New England. When told of the Long Cruise he smiled broadly and declared, "This is one man we're going to talk with." They remained nearly an hour.

He mentioned the "Missing Link," the section between the Green Mountains in Vermont and the White Mountains in New Hampshire, which had been wrecked by a hurricane ten years before. He hadn't had time to reopen it yet but hoped I could get through. I assured him it couldn't be any worse than some sections in the South. He and his co-workers, volunteering time and effort to build and maintain the Appalachian Trail, were typical of the "Trail People," that incredible clan of thousands that made the dream of Benton MacKaye come true. I am proud to be one of them.

Insects, especially gnats, were pesky that afternoon. They danced by the dozens in front of my eyes, trying desperately to enter and drown in the resulting tears. I swatted lots of them, knocking myself silly, but others replaced those that "went west." The netting had long since worn out. At Dalton I tried to replace it but couldn't find any. I would have side-tracked to Pittsfield but a man at the bus stop said the stores would be closed by the time the bus got there. So I bought supplies in Dalton and moved along a mile or two before stopping to sleep at trailside. Beautiful, no rain.

At Cheshire I paused to examine the memorial to Elder John Leland, eulogized on the plaque as "Eloquent Preacher, Beloved Pastor, Influential Patriot, and Father of Religious Liberty." Also recorded was the fact that he helped elect President Jefferson and later presented the President, in the presence of assembled dignitaries, with the "Big Cheshire Cheese," weighing 1235 pounds. West of Cheshire is Hancock, once a Shaker Community. This religious sect was known for its celibacy, and for distinctive furniture and other handcrafted items.

From Cheshire the Trail ascended the Greylock Range, where I stopped to sleep at the leanto on Saddle Ball, in the dry for a change. Rain came at night and continued as far as the summit of Mt. Greylock, highest peak in Massachussetts at 3491 feet elevation. The Memorial there honors the sons and daughters of the state who served in wartime. A spiral stairway gives access to observation windows at the top. Several carloads of visitors arrived, and the children of one family trooped up the stairs and shouted to their mother who had stayed below. Clouds were settling into surrounding valleys, so that peaks barely showed. Occasionally a rift would

A war memorial honoring residents of Massachusetts crowns Mt. Greylock, the highest peak in the state.

show the adjacent lowlands. Into these go many ski runs, including the Thunderbolt, for experts only.

North of Greylock the Trail followed ski trails for miles, with marking alternating between circular insignia and the standard blaze. Bugs, meanwhile, were as bad as ever, and my first action at Blackinton was to get netting. None of the stores had any so I caught a bus to North Adams and was able, once again, to get some in a department store. After eating at a diner and mailing some cards I caught a return bus to Blackinton, arriving as a violent storm was breaking. While waiting under an awning in front of a grocery store, I talked with an aging baseball player who probably never did much else. He could describe in detail every game in which he had ever played. A few miles north of Blackinton is the state line of Vermont and the beginning of the Long Trail, which extends all the way to Canada. The Appalachian Trail follows it as far as Sherburne Pass before turning eastward.

Behind me now was the low-lying central part of the Appalachian Mountain System, passing close to large population centers yet surprisingly wild and interesting. It is there that the greatest effort is necessary to preserve what is left of the wilderness along the Trail. The encroachment that once seemed overwhelming must be stopped if the Appalachian Trail is to survive. Benton MacKaye once told me he had believed a trail, like a chain, was no better than its weakest link, but had changed his mind. The best way was to strengthen the weak links as much as possible.

The Long Cruise was now entering the higher, more rugged section of trailway, the counterpart of the Southern Highlands, with extensive National Forests, timberline peaks and ridges instead of the balds of the South, the Presidential Range instead of the Smokies, and Katahdin instead of Oglethorpe.

Mansions of Green

The Long Trail north over ridges green,
'Neath skies of bonny blue,
With many a sylvan lakeside scene
But sometimes rugged too.

MOVING ALONG FROM BLACKINTON, through brush still wet from the rain, I came in the twilight to Seth Warner Camp, a closed shelter with a chunk stove inside. One of the bunks even had a mattress. The night was rainy and it was nice to be under a roof. Next morning the Lone Expedition came to Camp Coomash, on the shore of Sucker Pond. This beautiful little lake is part of the water supply for the town of Bennington, in the westward valley. Sitting on the cabin porch was Bob Quackenbush, keeper of the reservoir. He was delighted to see me, and immediately put on the kettle for tea, reminding me of the New Zealanders in the South Pacific.

Bob had the look of one who is much alone, and attuned to the ways of nature. He showed paw marks on the wall of a raccoon that sometimes came inside. He laughed when told of the one in Palisades Park. His family lived in Bennington and he went there on weekends but stayed at the camp most of the time. It had been built by men from Coopers Machine Shop. One man who came by one day afterward sent a letter addressed to "The man who lives on the Mountain." The letter was delivered promptly. Bob said that Sucker Pond had originally flowed to the east, away from the town, but a seven-foot-high dam turned its outflow the opposite way. He rowed me out to take pictures.

After a while three boys came along and they hiked with me as far as Thendara Camp, where we met a man who was frantically slapping insects, and no wonder. He was wearing shorts and tennis shoes only, and had no bug dope. He was checking the shelter, intending to bring his nephew for an overnight stay, a clear case of the blind leading the blind. The boys, Charles Lesure, Don Haczynski, and Fred Tatro, turned back, while I continued on to Hamlin Hill, a fern-covered summit overlooking Bennington. During the Revolution the Green Mountain Boys fought there to prevent the

The Seth Warner Camp provided welcome shelter from another rainy night.
A new Seth Warner Shelter has since been built along this stretch of A.T.,
which follows Vermont's Long Trail.

British from capturing a powder house and other vital supplies in one of the crucial engagements leading to Burgoyne's surrender. The official flag of the United States, containing thirteen stars and thirteen stripes, was first flown in battle at Bennington. The town is also known for the beautiful old pottery made there, for the collection of Grandma Moses' paintings, and the display of Amberina glass in its museum.

From Hamlin Hill the Trail crossed Molly Stark Highway, then followed a brook to Fay Fuller Camp, a closed stone cabin containing two fireplaces. Someone had left some candles and magazines, a temptation that caused me to read until midnight and again in the morning before leaving. The dirt road beyond Fay Fuller Camp dwindled to a path up a ravine to Glastenbury Camp, where I stopped to cook. Two men came along, one a veteran who said he had been over the mountain at least a hundred times. The other was the bug man of the day before, now wearing a shirt and using bug dope. A few miles farther was Caughnawaga Shelter, built by Boy Scouts and presented to the Green Mountain Club. Later I stopped to photograph the stone marker at the spot where Daniel Webster stood when addressing a Whig Party gathering in 1840. About 15,000 people attended. A colorful sunset was flaming high as I reached Webster Shelter, on the slope of Stratton Mountain. The water supply was difficult to find, and swampy. Black flies were bad, but held in check with a smudge fire.

The "bug man" and a veteran hiker stopped by to chat at Glastenbury Camp.

Fire Warden Barrett came along in the morning and we walked up the mountain together. He said that fishing was good in Stratton Pond and offered some line and hooks, which I declined with thanks. Fishing and long distance hiking don't combine very well. The top of Stratton Mountain affords a fine view of the Green Mountains north and south, and Benton MacKaye told me he was perched in a tall tree on the summit when he got the definite idea for the Appalachian Trail.

A Mr. Hinkle and two boys came by and walked along with me to Stratton Pond, where a youngish couple was staying at the lodge. The little lady declared she had long wanted to hike the A.T. all-the-way, and asked a lot of questions. The man, who was as big as she was little, stood by frowning. Mr. Hinkle and the boys turned back, while I started around the lake. The man and woman were quarreling before I was beyond earshot. At Stratton View Shelter I was sitting on the "Deacons Bench," the cross timber at the lower front of the leanto, pondering whether to stop early, when a rowboat started from the lodge, rowed clumsily by the little lady. The man was coming around by shore. When they got there I was gone.

At Bourn Pond a deer was out in the shallows, pulling up and eating water lilies. Porcupines were gnawing at an abandoned house nearby, making sounds similar to a "horse fiddle," that horrendous noisemaker often used in the old days at shivarees. The porcupine is also despised for an obvious reason, those nasty quills. In the twilight I arrived at Swezey Camp, an abandoned and rundown loggers'

Daniel Webster is immortalized at a site on the south side of Stratton Mountain. A colorful sunset was "flaming high" at the nearby Webster Shelter.

camp. The door was about to fall off and the stove pipe was missing, which wasn't all bad, since the smoke discouraged insects. Supper was cooking, more or less, when a scratching came at the door and a beady eye peaked round the door. Then old porky himself strutted in, with every quill raised. My verbal invitation to leave was ignored so I ushered the critter out with a stick.

Down the Trail a short distance in the morning I met an old man and his two grandsons. They had been on a fishing trip, staying at a place near Swezey Camp, and were going home to Manchester Depot. Needing supplies, I tagged along. The old gentleman owned some of the woodlands we passed. We discussed the various trees, their values, and the methods of getting them out of the woods. Back on the Trail I came to Snow Valley, an elaborate skiing center, with runs downhill on the western slope, then came to a cross-mountain highway under construction. A car was parked there and two young men were stowing gear in the trunk. They had been working on the road, and staying at Bromley Lodge, but couldn't dig straight post holes and decided to quit before they were fired. They were going back to the lodge for more gear so we walked together. Then they decided to celebrate meeting me by cooking a last meal before leaving.

The way those college fellers started a fire was a sight to behold, from a distance. First pour some gasoline from a bottle into a dish, dump it into the chunk stove, and back off while lighting a match. The result was a ball of fire, a roar, and a dancing stove. After recovering my power of speech I told them they wouldn't start many fires that way. The food they produced would have fed a small army; then out came dishtowels, brillo pads, scouring powder, and various

Stratton Mountain hovers above Stratton Pond. It was on this peak in Vermont that Benton MacKaye first thought of an Appalachian Trail.

other aids to successful housekeeping. No wonder they needed two trips to carry out their gear.

Bromley Ski Resort had many trails into the valley, some with colorful and appropriate names, such as "Twister" and "Shin-cracker." At the top was an essential part of any ski center, the first aid station. I peeked in a window and noted that a porcupine had chewed a hole in the floor, a favorite way of gaining entry. The usual ski lifts extended to the valley. Downhill skiing is almost like flying—very enjoyable—if you don't have to come back up the hard way.

North of Bromley Mountain was a section of Green Mountain National Forest, a picturesque region of heavy timber and isolated peaks. Shelters in the Forest were built of massive logs and three of them were spaced within ten miles. The first was Mad Tom and the second Griffith Lake, where another porcupine approached boldly while I was cooking and wasn't easy to chase away. At that time they were protected and had become a pesky nuisance. Since then their status has changed and they are not as numerous now.

For almost a week the weather had been good, practically a record. The morning sky was vivid blue, spotted with billowy clouds. Sometimes the path crossed swampy spots on corduroy, unlike so many places where you just slog through. After Old Job Shelter the Trail crossed a scenic highway and followed a woods road to Little Rocky Pond. Except for the easy access this is one of the nicest spots along the A.T. The lake was fringed with evergreens and the water was azure blue, said to be so deep that the bottom has never been

"One of the nicest spots along the A.T." is Little Rocky Pond. The shelter, no longer there, was on a small rocky island, reached by a wooden footbridge.

found. The leanto was on a small rocky island, reached by a rustic wooden footbridge, and facing the open lake. The lake was classed as experimental fishing waters and was stocked with rainbow trout.

Midafternoon shadows were slanting across the rippling waters when I finally persuaded myself to leave. This place tempted me to break my rule of traveling every day. I have been back several times, once staying overnight when a full moon was shining and wind clouds were crossing the sky. Greenwall Shelter was only five miles away but marking was faded and I made a wrong turn, finally arriving at the leanto by starlight. The spring was several hundred yards away and difficult to find in the dark. Next day I met people coming in to White Rocks, a high lookout, then crossed abandoned farms and a wide intervale to Buffum Shelter. Some fishermen had just finished dinner and were about to leave. One was toting a half empty jug of "stonefence" cider, which I politely but firmly refused to sample.

After cooking my own dinner I cruised past an abandoned lumber camp and over a ridge to Clarendon Gorge. The choice here was to descend and cross the canyon or detour to a flimsy footbridge. A regular suspension bridge has since been built but often is damaged by spring floods. I crossed the gorge, not trusting the footbridge, and came to Clarendon Shelter. A man was sitting there, reading a book. He was interested in my boots, said he had never found any that withstood the grueling conditions of trail travel and was currently trying paratrooper boots. Much of his hiking had been

It was hard to pull away from Little Rocky Pond, a setting of azure blue water ringed by dense evergreens.

in Maine, where footgear gets a real workout. Since Governor Clement Camp was only six miles away I didn't stay.

In late evening, while on a stretch of Trail along a brook where high water had washed out the path, I was surprised by a large mink and her kits, scattering into the brush. But one remained on the path, twitching its nose and watching me with beady eyes. The mother clucked anxiously from behind some driftwood but the kit wouldn't go. The lighting was poor but I tried for a picture anyway. When the shutter clicked that little rascal ducked as though it had been shot at, crawled under some weeds, opened its mouth wide, and began to squall and squeal. Out came the mother, quick as a flash, jumped over to the little one to make sure it wasn't hurt, jumped back in the brush and clucked some more. The kit just lay there and screeched. The second time the mother came directly, with obvious intent. As she leaped toward me I caught her on the nose with the toe of my boot, turning her over. Up came her tail and she turned on the spray, like her cousin the skunk would have done, gathered her litter, including the squealer, and herded them away without a backward glance. My clothes smelled minky for several days. It wasn't funny to her but it was to me.

Near sundown I came to a nice stone leanto, name forgotten. In the morning the grass and brush were wet and my clothes and gear needed attention so the start was delayed. I took time to restitch the boots and apply dubbing, sew a ripped pants leg with the baseball stitch, and take up the pack straps a little. Such a routine occasionally helps keep things together. By noon I had crossed the flank of Killington Peak and come to Coopers Lodge, a nice stone cabin honoring Charles P. Cooper. A man and a woman came up the side trail from the direction of Rutland, on their way to the summit. Then I caught up with three boys and walked with them until an approaching thunderstorm sent us in headlong flight to Long Trail Lodge in Sherburne Pass.

Knowing the Appalachian Trail turned eastward from Sherburne Pass, and finding no marking, I started on the highway. The storm became a cloudburst and muddy torrents soon were rushing down the roadside. Still seeing no marking, I decided to follow the road around to Gifford Woods State Park, through which the Trail definitely passed. There I signed the register, then talked to Grace Barrows, the first and only lady Ranger met on the Long Cruise. She told me that the leantos in the Park were available at a nominal fee. But several hours of daylight remained and I decided to keep going. Mrs. Barrows misunderstood and always blamed herself for my going. She told me years later that she never charged a through-hiker after that, regardless of regulations. This Park had the reputation of being one of the finest and best kept in the U.S.

Actually, I should have stayed. Faint blue marking at the highway indicated the beginning of the "Missing Link," the hurricane-wrecked and nearly obliterated section east from Sherburne Pass. The cloudburst had flooded the meadow, with water knee high on the stream bank and waist deep when I waded across. Beyond the meadow a sign at a road pointed toward the village of Sherburne. On the far side of the village a boy was playing in puddles. When asked about the Trail he referred me to the hired man, who was in the barn milking the cows. The hired man sent me to the grandfather of the house, a bright-eyed old man with a snowy thatch of hair who told me the Trail probably turned between there and Sherburne. Meanwhile the lady of the house had noticed my wet clothes and weary condition and urged me to stay overnight, seconded by the grandfather, who said the storm was not really over. How right he was. But I was bound to go on, not wanting to impose.

A faint blaze on a tree marked the turn up an old woods road up a ravine. Blowdowns and brush began to obstruct the path, as twilight deepened. It was time to stop. Finding a flat place by an old stump I set up the half wigwam shelter and started a fire against the stump, while rain began falling again. Spruce boughs were gathered to keep me off the wet ground. The fire was difficult to start but set the stump on fire and was difficult to put out in the morning. During that dreary night I heard for the second time in my life the awesome sound of a giant tree falling somewhere in the stillness. Long dead, and weighted by soaking rain, it had finally crumbled. This is something that many lifelong woodsmen have never heard. Now I knew why I hadn't stayed at Sherburne.

The "Missing Link," a hurricane-wrecked section east of Sherburne Pass, Vt., required wading across a flooded meadow. The rains continued during the night, felling a giant tree "somewhere in the stillness."

Next day the woods road dwindled to an overgrown path and then dense thickets and young timber, with marking faint but traceable. On the far side of the ridge someone had crashed through with a jeep, which helped. Finally I came to a sawmill clearing and was astonished to see an old trail sign on a loggers shack, designating "Notown Camp." It looked as though porcupines had been the only occupants for years. The woods beyond had been nearly clear-cut a few years before, resulting in dense growth, but a faint blue blaze every mile or so kept me going down a long straight valley eastward. Then marking disappeared and the only way to proceed was by dead reckoning, compass in hand, which brought me to Barnard Gulf Road, near the Trail crossing.

From this point the Trail was maintained by Dartmouth Outing Club and was in better shape, except that their marking, alternate red and white bands, was faded and difficult to identify. At night I stopped at a ramshackle barn, found some hay in a mow, and slept there during a thunderstorm. Had a strong wind come with the storm I would have moved out, since the structure looked ready to collapse. Because of wet brush and lack of marking, I followed a country road past Pomfret to West Hartford and intercepted the Trail there. Marking was better beyond and so was the weather, with progress more rapid to Norwich. First stop, as usual, was the grocery store. For the first time powdered milk was available, which meant a slight saving in weight. Before this my milk was canned.

My arrival at Norwich had been too late to pick up mail so I crossed the Connecticut River and continued through Hanover, missed the turnoff to Velvet Rocks Shelter in the darkness and slept in a roadside woods, returning to Norwich in the morning. At least I had gotten the "Missing Link" behind me and it hadn't been as bad as expected. My equipment was showing definite signs of wear, and so was I. The moccasin boots were cracked and misshapen but holding together. The framepack was smoke stained and getting shabby. The cookkit was dented and black on the outside. The poncho was faded and slightly torn. The rainhat was floppier than ever. The burlap bag was black on one side from wrapping around the cookkit. As Whittier said of the Deacon's Masterpiece, there was "a general flavor of mild decay but nothing local as one might say."

Still ahead of me were some of the most rugged and remote sections of trailway, over the timberline in the White Mountains and through the wilderness of Western Maine. But in many ways this kind of travel is easier than the backyard wilderness variety, where the best route is often not available. The nasty dogs and the four-lane highways are few and far between, but so are the grocery stores. Poison snakes are no longer a threat but bear and moose can be under sudden circumstances, and insects can be exceedingly obnoxious. Yet these are a part of the free wild way of the wilderness, the natural hazards.

Mountains of the Snowy Foreheads

On the threshold of outer silence,
Where the winds above timberline blow
And sunclouds are rivalled in brilliance
By the glittering summertime snow.

THE HIGHLANDS OF NEW HAMPSHIRE have a bleak ruggedness that commands the respect of the hardiest mountaineer. Some of the worst weather on earth occurs here, with winds of more than gale velocity and temperatures of polar intensity. Freezing weather is possible in midsummer and a snowstorm can follow hot weather within an hour. Almost all weather tracks known to the North American continent converge here, from Greenland or Hudson Bay, from the Great Lakes, from the Appalachian Valleys, and from the Coastal Atlantic. The results can be overwhelming. Many people have died because they didn't know or ignored these facts. Precautions should always be taken. Scanty clothing should never be worn above timberline and emergency rations and gear should be carried.

The Indians called the White Mountains "Agiochook," "Mountains of the Snowy Foreheads." They never ascended the highest summits, believing them to be the abode of the Great Spirit, and that anyone who climbed there would be doomed to wander forever with no hope of reaching the Happy Hunting Ground. Yet one legend told of a man and wife who climbed Mt. Washington to escape a terrible flood, and returned to repopulate the land. Today the area is mostly National Forest, criss-crossed by foot trails, and visited by millions of people.

After crossing the Connecticut River on the highway bridge from Norwich, the Trail passed through Hanover past the Dartmouth College campus. This school was originally founded to train missionaries to the Indians and the Indians themselves. From Hanover the Trail turned upward to Velvet Rocks Shelter, where I cooked a belated breakfast. Beyond were fields and woods to Moose Mountain, and then more fields and woods to the foot of a steep slope, where the Trail forked. Signs indicated alternate routes. Naturally I chose the more scenic and longer route to Holts Ledge Cabin, situated in the sag between the ledge and Bear Hill. The cabin was supposed to be locked but someone had broken in. Porcupines were numerous there but hadn't managed to enter, probably because the logs were creosoted.

This was the first good stopping place since the Long Trail and I took my time in the morning, getting shipshape before leaving. At Smarts Mountain the Trail turned to bypass the crest toward Cube Mountain, which had been hopelessly snarled by the hurricane. While on the bypass route I came around a bend and saw two backpackers sitting on a bridge over a brook. They were Jimmy Calloway and Paul Yambert, two husky Tennesseeans who had started from Katahdin the first of June in an attempt to get through to Oglethorpe. They looked like toughened bush-walkers, capable of going all the way, but inclined to carry too much, in the opinion of various people I talked to later. Eventually Jimmy and Paul went as far as Central Virginia before hearing I had finished and deciding to go back to college. Three years were to go by before Gene Espy duplicated my south-to-north trip, and Chester Dziengielewski and Martin Papendick completed the trip north-to-south the same year.

The summit of Cube Mountain has twin tops, with boulders and spruce thickets between. I heard shouting ahead and found a group of boys at the leanto. They carefully explained they were thirteen and fourteen year olds from Camp Moosilauke, bunk seven, senior hill. Their counselor was Bert Fredericks, student at Indiana College, now working over the summer. They insisted I stay and have supper with them. I knew I shouldn't but did. It was a hectic affair of burned raw potatoes, black-red hamburgers, and hastily heated beans, using my cooking grease and kettles, two incidentals they had forgotten to bring. The leanto was useless, its floor half eaten by porkies, so all hands slept in the bush. The boys were noisy all night, the usual way of greenhorns, and I left at daybreak, not expecting to see them again, but they barged past later, waving and yelling. At least they would get a well-cooked breakfast at camp.

The DOC Camp at Lake Armington was accessible by automobile and therefore much used. Another favorite was Wachipauka Pond. The path to the road was well worn. Bob Lapierre and his nephew were going in for a swim. He invited me to stay at his camp near Glencliff, saying he would drive me to the camp from the village and bring me back in the morning. I agreed but shouldn't have. The camp was too much like an army barracks and Bob was late in getting me back to the Trail, not seeming to realize how important an hour or two can be to a distance hiker.

The five-mile drag up Moosilauke took more than three hours, bringing me for the first time above true timberline. The trees got shorter and shorter until they were only scattered clumps the size of

It took more than three hours to climb the five miles up to the top of Mt. Moosilauke. At the edge of timberline was a Dartmouth Outing Club cabin. The cabin, now gone, was painted like an old DOC blaze. Above timberline was an all-rock summit and a view of the Presidentials.

bushes. The summit was almost nothing but acres of rocks. At the edge of timberline, near a rock cranny spring, was a shelter, bolted and cabled to the rocks because of the violent winds that occur there. This is a world of silence. Even a strong wind makes little noise when not obstructed. The view from Moosilauke is far-reaching across the Presidentials, the dominant range in the Northern Appalachians, when the weather is good. A large resort hotel once stood on the topmost point of the peak, reached by a carriage road up the long spur from Glencliff, but it had burned years before in a lightning fire. I regretted not having kept on to the high shelter the evening before.

Above timberline the Trail was marked by stone cairns, with trail signs on short posts wedged into the rocks. The cairns are close enough to be followed during foggy or snowy weather. This first time above timberline gave me a strange feeling, as though it were possible to fall off the earth. Beyond the summit were high spruce bogs, where I met a man who was hiking from Lost River to the Ravine House, located on a side trail. The outflow from the bog dropped down the far side of Moosilauke as Beaver Brook, actually a series of cascades and falls most of the way to Lost River Canyon. The Trail followed closely and was very treacherous, slippery with spray and very steep over broken terrain. Crude ladders made passage possible at some points. In Kinsman Notch I missed the shelter, which must have been on an unmarked side trail, and started out Kinsman Ridge.

This section had been storm wrecked and hadn't been cleared for years. I should have stopped but hoped for a shelter ahead and

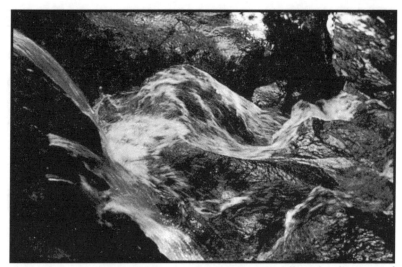

Down from the summit of Mt. Moosilauke, the A.T. followed a slippery and steep course adjacent to Beaver Brook. The tributary cascaded and fell most of its way to Lost River Canyon.

kept on through cloudy darkness until my leg was almost broken by colliding with a log. The only way then was to crawl under a dense spruce tree and reach up for boughs to make a bed. Luckily, no rain came. Eliza Brook Shelter was about a half mile beyond and breakfast was cooked there. Next came Mt. Kinsman, steep sloped and strewn with down trees. Sometimes cracks showed in the rocks, as though a landslide was imminent. No blaze marking was used on Appalachian Mountain Club trails at that time and destination signs were often missing or defaced. So it wasn't surprising that I turned wrong at a trail that came out to Cannon Mountain instead of Lonesome Lake. Cannon Mountain is a deluxe skiing center, complete with an aerial tramway, the first one in America. It brought people to the summit in a few minutes, almost like an elevator in a tall building.

Tourists were strolling about the summit or staring across Franconia Notch to Mt. Lafayette, a towering peak scarred by several landslides, one of them less than a week old. I kept apart, being oriented to the wilderness, poignantly aware of the difference between the world of nature and the feverish holiday atmosphere of crowds who seem to dread venturing far from automobiles, restaurants, and deluxe cable cars. My descent of Cannon Mountain by shoe leather express took about an hour.

A man in Franconia Notch told me that Greenleaf Trail ascended to Greenleaf Hut on Lafayette, intercepting the A.T. there, but starting up so late was not advisable, since the slide had torn out a

The Greenleaf Hut provided hospitable respite before the rest of the climb up Mt. Lafayette, towering behind it. It was also where I first met the Biddle brothers, fellow Pennsylvanians, "practically neighbors."

part of the Trail. It had started high up in the usual way, a boulder or two breaking loose and starting a chain reaction of rocks, trees, and earth ripping a great white gash in the mountainside, almost to the highway in the Notch. When I got that far some footprints indicated others had crossed the slide so I did likewise, pausing midway to snap a picture of the Great Stone Face, jutting prominently from the side of Cannon Mountain. This awesome natural wonder, immortalized by Nathaniel Hawthorne, is seen by many thousands of people from Profile Clearing in Franconia Notch.

Black flies were bad so I broke off a spruce bough and was absent-mindedly waving it over my head when arriving at Greenleaf Hut. Two young men, pitching horseshoes back of the hut, stared at me and my spruce bough. "I'm not bushed, just allergic to flies," I assured them hastily. They were Bill and Craig Biddle, from Philadelphia, practically neighbors of mine. Then Ed Hertzberg, of Yellow Springs, Ohio, came out and asked if I was staying overnight. He and his wife were taking a mountaineer vacation for the first time in ten years. While we were talking Pete Walker, at least six and a half feet tall and hailing from Washington, D.C., came in, followed by Dave Cressler, of North Conway, Mass., and Don Grout, of Irvington-Hudson. When told that I would be moving on a mile or two before stopping for the night they looked up at the rocky upper reaches of Lafayette, almost obscured by threatening clouds, and reckoned that wasn't a good idea. I finally had to admit that a temporary lack of funds was the reason. Ed Hertzberg immediately offered to pay, but the hut crew huddled and came up with this remarkable document:

Attention, All Huts:

This man has already walked 1700 miles of the Appalachian Trail and is about to do the last 300 of it. We at Greenleaf, in view of his tremendous accomplishment, feel that Joe would be only too willing to deadhead him through any of the Huts in the system. We know that you will all follow suit in aiding him to reach the end of his trail.

> *Pete Walker, Hutmaster*
> *Dave Cressler, Assist.*
> *Don Grout, Crew*

My offer to forward payment later was firmly rejected. Ed remarked that the proper way was to pass the favor along to some-one else. Wouldn't it be a nice world if everyone had that philosophy? Even though mealtime was long past the crew insisted on cooking a special supper, while the talk was constant and enthusiastic. The hullabaloo finally subsided and all hands retired to dormitory cots. To realize the implications of their hospitality one must understand that supplies for these lofty hostels were brought by donkey pack train or backpacked by the crew themselves. These young men, usually college students, handled the chores of the hut system, cooking, ship-shaping, and handling pedestrian traffic. Their capabilities and dedication are legendary. Many prominent citizens were formerly crewmen.

Rain fell during the night, as expected, and continued through early morning, with Lafayette swathed in ominous cloud. After washing the dishes we waited around for a break in the weather. The Biddles were the first to go, heading for Profile Clearing. Then the Hertzbergs left for Lonesome Lake, leaving me to face the cloudswept timberline. The hut crew came out to watch and bid me "Have a good trip," as I shouldered the smoky old pack and even picked up the spruce bough where it had been left by the door. I've often wondered what those guys were thinking as they watched me climbing that rocky peak into the clouds.

The Trail now crossed barren rocks, mile after mile. Clouds trailed by haphazardly but the rain had stopped except for occasional squalls. Visibility was poor but the cairns kept me from getting lost. This was my first real taste of timberline, for hours at a time. Midafternoon brought me to Galehead Hut, where a crewman immediately heated water for tea. Yodels drifted down from nearby heights and the crew went outside to answer. I met the party soon after starting on and they looked very tired. The rain quickened as I reached a timely haven at Zeacliff Shelter, located by a small lake near towering cliffs. My bed was traditional, a thatch of spruce boughs. Meanwhile some marsh peepers were sounding along the lake, their silver voices blending with rain on the roof in a wilderness lullaby.

The hut crew at Zealand Falls had left a note on the door saying they were out for supplies. I photographed the nearby falls before moving through Zealand Notch, which is more like a sag, extending several miles and encompassing the headwaters of the Pemigewasset River. One pool looked especially inviting and the cool water was soothing to my strap-chafed shoulders and rock-jolted feet. The last few miles to Willey House Station crossed boggy plateau, then dropped abruptly to the little old railroad station in Crawford Notch.

The post office was already closed, making a stayover necessary, since I was expecting a money order. I was pitching camp beyond the highway near a stream when two women approached. One looked very tired and disgruntled. She vehemently advised me not to cross the next mountain, that they had spent the whole day on a terrible trail. When I mentioned already having walked from Georgia, she stopped talking and stared. The younger woman then asked questions about obtaining supplies and the hazards of traveling alone. Soon the rest of their party came up, some of them in a state of collapse. The man in charge was relieved to learn they were so close to Willey House.

The next day was remarkably beautiful, billowy clouds in a deep blue sky, perfect for hiking and photography. Unfortunately my film supply was very low. After stopping at the post office for the letter, which had come as expected, I began a hectic effort to hitchhike to North Conway. No one would stop, probably because I didn't have my pack along. Then a car finally stopped. In it were two fashionably dressed young women, who seemed willing to let me ride despite my trailworn appearance. They made room among the baggage on the back seat and took me aboard. The driver remarked, "Mama had misgivings about my touring the White Mountains until assured that no foolhardy hiking would be attempted." The other girl probably was her chaperone and companion. They insisted on stopping wherever film might be available, even at roadside stands, until we reached North Conway, where some was available; and they waved and smiled as they traveled on.

No kind-hearted damsels came from the opposite direction. Several hours passed before a man took me as far as Bartlett. I started walking after another hour there, even though the distance to the notch would have taken the rest of the day and all night. This changed my luck. A crew of road workers took me all the way to Willey House. The sun was halfway down as I resumed the trek over Webster Cliff Trail. Once I spotted a spruce hen hiding among some stunted spruce, its natural color making it difficult to see. Just before sunset I rounded a knoll and saw a leanto at the head of a long southerly ravine. Two movements caught my eye, one by the shelter, one by the spring. It was Bill and Craig Biddle, just arrived. Oddly enough, I had been thinking about them that day, wondering if we

The Biddles were already at the Mizpah Shelter and there was a festive reunion. What had been the most primitive and remote shelter along the A.T. in the White Mountains has since been replaced by a most elaborate structure.

would meet again. Bill said later that they were discussing the same thing. They said they wouldn't have wanted to meet anyone else, and the feeling was mutual.

This was Mizpah Shelter, with a good sweetwater spring and a long southern view, the most primitive and remote shelter along the Trail in the White Mountains. We decided to celebrate by splurging on food. They had a can of peaches they had been hoarding for days, and some powdered soup. One of my contributions was panbread. Bill watched me mix flour, oatmeal, and cornmeal at random, toss in salt and baking powder, mix with water, then toss the mixture into the pan well-greased with margarine, and flip it over when it was done on one side. Bill watched in fascination and said I ought to call it "Wonder Bread," because he wondered what it would taste like and also whether it would land in the pan coming down. That's what it's been ever since. Best part is, it never tastes quite the same.

The night was cold and windy so I slept on the bough bed in the shelter. Bill and Craig had warm sleeping bags and preferred the outside. In the morning we talked a while before leaving, once again in opposite directions. A white-throated sparrow was singing nearby and Bill wrote years later that he always thought of Mizpah Shelter when he heard one. One thing is certain. We'll never see Mizpah again, as it was then. That leanto has been replaced by the most

In between Mt. Monroe and Mt. Washington (background) was Lakes of the Clouds Hut which was undergoing renovation. Nearby were glacial ponds and, despite the warm temperature of a sunny July day, two patches of snow.

elaborate hut in the White Mountains. Seventeen years later, when southbound, I didn't even stop for a drink of water, and turned on the wrong trail. The people were tourists, not hikers.

From Mizpah I crossed Mt. Pleasant and Mt. Franklin, to the summit of Mt. Monroe and a fine view of Mt. Washington, highest peak in the northern Appalachians at 6288 feet elevation. In the notch between was Lakes of the Clouds Hut. The glacial ponds nearby are the highest in New England. Off to the right, in sharp contrast to moss and lichen covered rocks, were two patches of snow, even though this was a sunny day in July. I turned aside for a closeup look and pictures. Lakes of the Clouds Hut was being remodeled and enlarged, the materials brought in by backpackers. A few years later it would have been helicopters.

I talked briefly with the hut crew, then started for the summit, catching up with a man and his two small sons and slowing to walk with them. He said he was taking it easy, doubtful that the boys could make it. Half an hour later they were scampering far in front and he was laboring hard. He wasn't that old, just out of shape, and the timberline was telling him so.

The cog railway train had just arrived, and several cars had come on the toll road, so the summit was swarming with people. When the railroad was first proposed, about a hundred years earlier, the idea was ridiculed with an offer for a franchise to build a railroad to the moon. The toll road is almost as unbelievable, and rough on vehicles. But most people will pay to ride, rather than walk, even to the top of a mountain. A weather station has long been located on the summit of Washington. Wind velocities of several hundred miles an hour have been recorded, and midsummer snows have occurred, lasting as long as a week and dropping as much as ten feet of snow. The extremes probably result from the high location between the warm Gulf Stream in the Atlantic and the Arctic reaches of Canada. Only Katahdin rivals and possibly surpasses Washington in weather extremes.

The Appalachian Trail curves along the crest of the Presidential Range, always well above timberline, instead of taking the easier and shorter route down Tuckerman Ravine. Hikers were numerous. Once a group of college girls came along and I stepped aside. Most were too weary to notice anything except the rocks at their feet, but a few smiled shyly. Later I overtook two young men from Minnesota, one of them tall, red-headed, and the most stumble-footed hiker I have ever seen. Perhaps it was his hobnailed boots. He sprawled repeatedly but always managed to avoid breaking bones. The prospect of helping carry out a casualty didn't appeal to me so I wasn't sorry when they turned off on a side trail.

The sun was low as I crossed Mt. Adams and came to Madison Springs Hut, signed the register and talked with the crew, telling them I would cross Madison before stopping.

Outside the hut Ward Hinkson, of Chester, Pennsylvania, deliberately introduced himself and asked what I was doing. He was a long-time hiker who had climbed every important peak in the Adirondacks at least once and was now planning to climb them again with his sons. Ward was at Katahdin weeks later when my trip ended. Of special interest at Madison huts were the donkeys and burros stabled there. They were used to pack most of the supplies to the various huts. The wrangler said they were all right when you could get them to move. The army once tried to outdo them with army pack mules but failed miserably. I had to suppress a pernicious notion to borrow one of the long-eared critters.

The sun was setting as I scrambled over Madison but light lingers long above timberline. Valleys already were in black shadow and the soundless twilight of the high country was deepening as I reached a spring in the first fringe of timber. My bed was a mat of spruce needles back of a rock. The Trail was only a few feet away but the average person would never have spotted me. When I left, the signs of my presence were so slight that the next rain would remove them. Like the Indians, I say "Where I go I leave no sign."

Three big and husky young men came striding, soon after I started. One suggested, condescendingly, that carrying an axe really wasn't necessary. I didn't bother to tell him how far I had come, but did mention that some parts of the Appalachian Trail were vastly different from New Hampshire. He shrugged indifferently and the three strode nonchalantly on. It is for such as these that the warning signs are placed at timberline.

Pinkham Notch Hut was headquarters for Joe Dodge, Hut Manager and mountaineer of vasty reputation. One of the crew took me to his office, mentioning on the way that you only need to get within a hundred yards to meet Joe. This could be exaggeration, but the "Paul Bunyan" of the White Mountains did have a booming voice and a knack for storytelling. Many "Goofers" have heard his tales of "Green-eyed Comatabodys" and suchlike monsters Joe had met in the wilds. His rescue efforts were legendary. He was the leader in developing the Hut System in the White Mountains for the Appalachian Mountain Club. We talked for about an hour, with footgear as a main topic. Joe favored leather soles and calks, while my preference is for composition soles.

Pinkham Notch Hut, unlike the others, is located near the highway in the Notch, with vacationers lounging about on porches and lawns. They took scant notice of the lone hiker passing on the way to the Wildcat Range. A mile or so beyond the highway was Lost Pond, with its series of beaver dams, with water between. Each would slow the leakage in dry weather and lessen the pressure in time of flood, an incredible bit of animal engineering. To the south was Glen Ellis Falls, where water tumbles violently down a fissure in a cliff.

The climb from Pinkham Notch was very steep, on a series of shelves and ledges. Near the top a man came headlong, slowing himself by grabbing bushes and trees. He stopped long enough to introduce himself as "MacInnes, a chemist," and to assure me there was "Plenty of swamp water" on the Wildcat. I learned afterward that this man was internationally known as a scientist and almost as well known for his mountaineering. The swamp water he referred to was sometimes in rock basins and usually "alive."

From cliffs on Wildcat Mountain an overlook shows the hut in Carter Notch directly below, near two small lakes, and the Trail snakes down the cliff. The crewman on duty put the kettle on for tea while telling me his partner was due back with a packload. A few minutes later a crack-voiced yodel announced his arrival. He was big and husky but staggering. He said, when able to talk, that he would never make two pack trips in one day again. They tried to give me supplies but I had enough to reach Gorham and wanted to travel as lightly as possible. They said that Imp Shelter was a long way off and I might as well stay the night. I didn't dare show them the letter from the Greenleaf Crew or they never would have let me go. As it was they cheerfully bid me "Have a Good Trip" while stuffing chocolate bars and other goodies into my pack before I could escape.

Imp Shelter was indeed far off, beyond Carter Dome, Middle Carter, and North Carter. Cloud fog closed in like a snowy ocean,

The A.T. now bypasses the town of Gorham, N.H. Beyond are the Mahoosucs, and memories of a night-time bout with "downright vicious" mosquitoes.

with high points for islands. When night came I might as well have been blind. Somehow, probably because of my green eyes, I crept along but didn't reach the shelter until midnight. I struck a match to view the interior and saw a porcupine disappearing through a hole in the floor. A chunk stove and bough-thatched bunk provided comparative comfort. The fog was gone in the morning but a lack of destination signs caused me to miss Mt. Surprise and reach the highway several miles south of Gorham. The Trail, incidentally, now goes that way. No one in Gorham, not even the lady in the information booth, seemed to know anything about the Trail. She did furnish a Forest Service map of the White Mountains and suggested the A.T. might cross the Androscoggin River at the power dam north of town. The town of Gorham is famous for the fine silver handcrafted there in years gone by.

Gorham was a mailing point, but this was Sunday and the post office was closed. The attendant at the power station was happy to have a visitor, said Calloway and Yambert had also stopped there. He mentioned a cold water spring a short distance up the Trail and I slept there. Mosquitoes were downright vicious, disregarding the "6-12" repellent I was using. On trips since then I always carry a headnet, the hooped kind, and consider it essential. At Pinkham Notch I could have and should have gotten some "Joe Dodge Special." It appeared to be the same formula used by Nessmuk many years before. It's wicked stuff but bugs don't like it either. The formula: one ounce of pennyroyal oil, two ounces of castor oil, and three ounces of pine tar, blended. Any bug that bites through that stuff has earned whatever he gets.

In the morning, I picked up mail, and finally had to ride a bus to Berlin to get color film. A girl on a seat in front told a friend she was home on a visit from her job in a restaurant in Shenandoah National Park. The man at Dales Radio Shop took a roll of film out of his own camera so I could have two. Back in Gorham I stocked up on food and got underway by early afternoon. Ahead was the Mahoosuc Range, not high but ranking as one of the toughest crossings on the entire A.T., with "plenty of ups and downs." Trident Shelter was shown on the map but had burned down. The next shelter was Gentian Pond, about five miles away. I practically ran through a region of swampy ponds, usually stained brown by rotting stumps and logs. Gentian Pond was one of the worst. Even the water in the brook was pretty rank. Otherwise the place was fine. A brilliant moon rose majestically and the air turned misty cool. The fire burned low and my thoughts were long of places and miles behind me, the changing mountain structure, the meetings with hundreds of people, and always the giant hills.

A section of untrodden Trail approached Goose Eye Mountain, the first high point in Maine. Full Goose Shelter appeared in a spruce clump on North Peak, but it was not yet time to call it a day.

Old Speck – Katahdin

*While the dawn of Summer season
cast a spell on western Maine,
O'er the lone lake-studded region
and the rock-peaked highland chain,
From the crest of Old Speck Mountain
on the wild Mahoosuc west
To the summit of Katahdin
and the ending of the quest.*

"Crossed the Maine-New Hampshire line about 2:15, 20th of July," says the Little Black Notebook. The morning was chilly, typical of full moon weather. The first high point beyond the line was Goose Eye Mountain, a rock dome almost devoid of vegetation. Yet a checkered adder, similar to the common garter snake, was sunning itself there. This was the last snake seen on the Long Cruise. Poisonous snakes are not encountered after reaching the White Mountains. Goose Eye is separated from North Peak by a narrow notch. On North Peak, in a spruce clump between boulders, was Full Goose Shelter, a nice spot, but Speck Pond was only five miles away. I was to learn that five miles can be a long, long haul in the state of Maine.

The Trail descended abruptly into a narrow boulder-clogged ravine, where temperatures dropped just as suddenly and ice appeared in crannies. This ice was yellow with age. For at least a mile the Trail threaded this strange labyrinth while the precious hours of daylight waned. This cleft in the mountain, known as Mahoosuc Notch, slanted slightly and a brook gradually formed, coming to a beaver pond, directly across the Trail, at the lower end. A large beaver swam boldly to the center of the pond, and ducked under while slapping its tail on the surface. This is the warning signal of the beaver and indicated this was a mother signaling her family. She repeated the maneuver several times. The pool was deep but I managed to wade along the edge and get by.

Beyond the pond was an abrupt turn up the mountain. I scrambled upward over rocks and projecting roots until marking faded on

Tree frogs guided me to the shore of Speck Pond and the old Speck Pond Shelter.

an open summit. Meanwhile, a rainstorm was definitely approaching and darkness was closing in. It seemed as though my only choice was to find shelter among the rocks. Then a sound, totally unexpected at such a place, solved the situation. The piping of tree frogs drifted up through the calm before the storm, and they could only be at Speck Pond. So—step by step through the cloudy darkness—I moved among rocks and thickets of spruce to the shore of the lake and followed it around to the shelter. Ever since, when the homeland meadows are turning green and the silvery lilt of those tiny peepers livens the night, I think of the time when they helped me "come to port" on the Long Cruise.

The bough bed inside the log leanto was a welcome couching place that night, as the rainstorm swept violently across Old Speck. Later the sky cleared and the late moon was reflected in the lake. Even the little frogs were silent then. With the dawn came a whirring sound in the woods, like two or three power saws, another species of frog serenading the sunrise. Speck Pond showed deeply blue within its border of spruce. It is said that the bottom of this lake, the highest in Maine, has never been found. Some people say it was caused by a falling meteor, but its location within a conical peak definitely indicates its origin was volcanic. Its overflow is down to Mahoosuc Notch through a great ravine or gulf in the side of Old Speck. This cleft continues through the notch and seems to extend all the way to the Great Gulf of Mt. Washington, as though a great explosion between the craters had cracked the earth. Old Speck is the third highest peak in Maine and second only to Katahdin in scenic beauty.

The Appalachian Trail circled the rimrock of Old Speck Mountain, over outcroppings of quartzite and other minerals mixed with granite, to the firetower on the highest point. I climbed up for a look around and to get aerial pictures of Speck Pond and Mahoosuc Notch. Rugged tops and ridges surround the peak, with the main extension of the White Mountains running northeast to Baldpate, Saddleback, and Sugarloaf. Part way down the far side I stopped at the Warden's Cabin to talk with Reggie Lord, a student at the University of Maine when not holding down the job of lookout on Old Speck. He said this tower was not popular because of the long steep climb out of Grafton Notch but he liked it because it kept him in shape for athletics.

Beyond Grafton Notch I side-trailed to Table Rock, then moved along to Baldpate, a dome-shaped peak just reaching timberline. There, for the first time, I encountered the drastic temperature change that can prevail at timberline. Above it I wore all my clothing and the poncho, below it all extra clothing had to be removed. Early stars were shining when I came to Frye Brook and groped through the darkening woods to the shelter. In the morning, when going back to photograph the waterfalls, the path skirted the rim of a miniature canyon at some places. Guess my guardian angel was with me that evening.

Beyond Andover Road was Elephant Mountain, remote and difficult to travel. Sometimes the Trail was on corduroy, left after logging in winter. The cross logs were left suspended when the snow melted, on stumps and slash, and now were beginning to rot. How hazardous this was can be imagined. Somewhere in all that tangled wilderness was an especially beautiful lake, where people had camped. Painted in blue on a rock was "God Bless Our Home."

Toward evening, I came to the shore of another lake at Camp Keewadin. Many waterfowl were floating or flying in the vicinity. Mosquitoes were vicious. At twilight the Lone Expedition came to Elephant Mountain Leanto. Cold weather socked in about midnight and morning brought dreary rain that lasted all day. The Trail was rough, with many blowdowns, some lengthwise on the path. By early evening I had progressed only eight miles to Sabbath Day Pond, where the roof of the leanto had collapsed so that water was running in instead of out. But the storm had become a real nor'easter, with a strong headwind, and stop I must. I managed to start a fire and cook what little food I had remaining, then wrapped in everything I had

Orbeton Stream marked the beginning of a section of Trail in Western Maine that had been closed because of hurricane damage. A sign warned: "Travel at your own risk."

under the poncho in the least wet corner of the leanto. There I stayed the rest of the day and all night, neither asleep nor awake, but in a kind of stupor. At dawn, a loon, first I had ever heard, began its echo-wailing and crazy laughter somewhere. Right then it seemed as though an utter pall of rain and melancholy had enwrapped the entire earth.

At such a place, without food, it was impossible to wait out the storm. Actually, it was almost over anyway. The rain eased as I traveled on, stopping once to watch a deer browse across the Trail ahead, then coming to a road crossing. My map indicated Rangely to the left. A bottled gas salesman soon came along and took me along to town, where I found a grocery store and also an information booth where a lady gave me an official map of Maine.

The town of Rangely, by the lake of the same name, is one of the better known resort centers of western Maine, with hotels and camps along the shore. Nearby is another lake called Mooselookmeguntic. I waited in front of the store and behold! the same gas serviceman came along and took me back to the Trail crossing, just as the man in the Model A had at Swatara Gap in Pennsylvania. My luck had changed, for the moment.

The terrain beyond the highway had been completely wrecked by the hurricane, with summer growth and brush growing through the fallen trees. Sometimes the going was easier in the woods parallel to the Trail. Conditions improved near Piazza Rock Leanto. The rock juts out so far that trees grow underneath as well as on top. Saddleback loomed high ahead, and conditions were good for a picture so I started up the slope, reaching the open crest in time to get a sunset picture over Rangely Lake. Beyond on the skyline were the Boundary Mountains, between Maine and Canada. Another picture a few minutes later shows the Trail crossing a rounded dome, with late sunlight streaking the picture, one of the best taken on the Long Cruise. After that I headed for the tree line and slept under some stunted spruce.

Breakfast was eaten at Popular Ridge Leanto. At Orbeton Stream a sign said, "Trail closed, in bad condition to Bigelow. Travel at your own risk." Blazes were gone, except for the original axe cuts, which could be followed as far as Spaulding Leanto, where I stopped to cook dinner, clearing away weeds in front of the shelter and even inside. Beyond was a mass of tangled down timber, grown through with summer growth. Sometimes I stumbled and fell headlong, the pack banging the back of my head. Once my knee missed a jagged rock by no more than an inch. Surely my guardian angel was with me that afternoon. Not even an ankle sprain resulted. Meanwhile the sky was chaotic, as though another violent storm was hovering over the wilderness. Getting stranded in this forsaken back country would have been disastrous.

Finally the Trail emerged on the open summit of Sugarloaf Mountain, second highest in Maine at 4237 feet. The two miles I had just hiked were the last to be completed of the original route in 1937. Right then it looked as though it had never been built at all. Chained to the topmost boulder on Sugarloaf was a bronze cylinder containing a register. Five people had signed it in as many years, two of them Jimmy Calloway and Paul Yambert. The leanto was on the far slope, and a large tree had fallen directly on the roof, leaving just enough space at one end for me to crawl in. What a relief it was to be through that hurricane wreckage.

The village of Bigelow, at the Carrabassett River, was almost deserted. I saw no one there. Bigelow Village and Sugarloaf Mountain are now a deluxe skiing center, greatly changed in appearance from 1948. The Trail beyond the village was passable, with several beaver ponds on the way to Horns Pond Leantos. A steep climb goes to the top of the Horns, which give an aerial view of the back trail. From there the route is on the crest of the Bigelow Range, with Bigelow Col as a deep notch separating the twin peaks of Bigelow. One of them has been renamed in honor of Myron Avery, and a memorial shelter is in the col.

The fire lookout in the tower of East Bigelow was a young man just out of high school. He said that a foot of snow was on the ground when he came on duty in the Spring and that strong winds often

The last mile of the original A.T. route was constructed to the summit of Sugarloaf Mountain. In 1948 it showed the scars of hurricane damage.

howled across the peaks at night but he still liked the job of lookout. The ridge was named for a Colonel Bigelow, who was with Benedict Arnold on the ill-fated expedition across Maine during the Revolution in an attempt to capture Quebec. Had this been successful Canada would probably be a part of the United States today. The expedition bogged down in the Dead River Valley, on the north side of the Bigelow Range. Much of the valley is now a backwater from a large dam.

    The Trail continued over Little Bigelow, coming down to the Ledge House, soon to be abandoned because of the dam. In the deep dusk I came to Jerome Brook Leanto, which had been flooded by a beaver dam several years before. Dynamiting the dam did no good. The beaver rebuilt it. They had to be live trapped and moved far away. Usually it is only the Trail and not a leanto that is flooded.

    In the morning, at West Carry Pond Camps, a lady was hanging out wash behind the big log lodge. She looked me over sharply, then invited me in for coffee and doughnuts, introducing herself in a roundabout way by saying Mr. Storey was away getting a boat he had bought and wouldn't be back before evening. As we sat in the big front room, facing the lake, a big mink darted out and scurried among the boats and canoes on the landing. Mrs. Storey told how Calloway and Yambert came by one rainy day. They were having a bad time. One had twisted his knee so badly he could hardly walk and the other had cut his hand with the axe. Their loads were heavy, which didn't help. Mrs. Storey said she would write "The Trail People"—first time I heard the term—and tell them about my coming by. They always stayed at the camps when trail-working in that area. Her daughter Louise, who had been fishing along the shore,

The village of Bigelow, now a deluxe ski center, was almost deserted. Beyond, the twin shelters and an A.T. sign were a welcome sight at the Horns Pond Leantos.

came in as I was about to leave. A week later, while in the new boat with her father, she caught a "togue"—local name for lake trout—that weighed sixteen pounds and was thirty-one inches long. It was so big and heavy she could hardly hold it for the picture they sent at Christmas time. Carry Pond evidently provides some very good fishing.

The first thing I saw at East Carry Pond was a pair of loons. A loon is somewhere between a wild goose and a penguin, both in appearance and performance. It is awkward on land and not too good at flying but is an expert swimmer, able to stay under water as long as five minutes, and apt to come up where you least expect. Its call is very distinctive, either a melodious echo-wailing or the cackling laughter for which it is best known. Loons prefer the far back lake country and will leave if too many people appear. At the camps on East Carry Pond I talked with F.D. Gaskell, the proprietor, and his family. He said this was called the Great Carrying Place, because the Old Canada Road, the Arnold Trail, and the Appalachian Trail all met there. Travelers up the Kennebec would make the short carries between the lakes and across to Dead River, which took them to the Boundary Mountains, where another carry took them across to Lake Megantic in Canada. The Gaskells invited me to stay at the camps but too much daylight remained and I moved along to Pierce Pond Leanto.

A loon wakened me in the morning and two deer fled when I went to the lake for water. The Trail came to Pierce Pond Camps and then followed the tote-road to the Kennebec River. A man came bouncing along in a buckboard and stopped to tell me about getting help if necessary to cross the river. The ancient phone at the river wouldn't work for me so I put myself across, in a boat, using the long shod pole, but ending a few hundred feet downstream on the far side. The Kennebec is a swift flowing stream with a rocky bottom. I've heard of other hikers who did a lot worse. After pulling the boat along the shore to the landing place, I still needed help in getting it back to the other side. Then someone started target shooting in a field nearby and I found a Maine guide and the District Fire Warden. They said they would take the boat back for me. The warden, considerably smaller than I, nonchalantly poled the boat across while the guide launched a canoe, stood upright in it and poled across with about five mighty heaves. The warden then crouched in the bow and was brought back just as speedily.

The guide walked along to Caratunk, stepped into the little restaurant when I entered, and announced, "This guy has walked all the way from Georgia." The few patrons glanced up, said nothing, and resumed eating. The proprietor of the nearby store was a real "down easter," taciturn but with a twinkle in his eye. When I had bought supplies and was about to leave he suddenly became talkative. The reason became apparent when a younger man suddenly dashed in the door. The storekeeper smiled slightly and said, "Be careful what you say now, he's from the paper." The grapevine telegraph had been busy. The resulting story appeared in the *Bangor News* and bulletins were carried on radio stations.

Beyond Caratunk the Trail followed the road for some distance. A truck driver stopped to offer a ride. When told I was honor bound to walk, he laughed and said, "I think I'd cheat once in a while." The Trail past Pleasant Pond was unpleasantly tangled with briers and swamp grass. I blundered through to the shore of Lake Moxie, opposite Troutdale Camps. Moxie is a long, narrow lake that gets its name from its brownish color. No one was at the boat landing but a fisherman came along in a canoe and offered to put me across. His name was Frank Wimmer. He was curious about my outfit, since he and a friend were planning a hiking trip. He resumed fishing after putting me ashore at Troutdale Camps. The A.T. has since been rerouted to eliminate this crossing of the lake. The brown water, incidentally, is only a few inches deep.

That night I slept under tall timber on the slope of Moxie Bald, while the hoo-HOO-hoo-HOO-ooo of a great horned owl was sounding close by. In the morning the Trail followed the curving strata of the mountain to the firetower on the summit. M.F. Spofford, of The Forks, Maine, was on duty. He often saw bears in berry patches when scanning with his binoculars but none appeared for my benefit. He showed me the rubber insulated stool he stood on to avoid being struck by lightning during storms. When I left the weather was perfect, with billowy clouds in the sky, the kind of conditions that make Maine a popular vacationland in Summer.

Ahead was a stretch of a hundred miles without shelters but with designated campsites. Leantos have since been built at most of them, usually by Louis Chorzempa. The Trail passed the village of Blanchard and then came to Monson, last town along the Trail in Maine. I stocked heavily on staples, bringing my pack weight to a whopping sixty pounds. A lady in the store offered me a ride as far as her home, which was declined. Then she came out to offer "lunch or a glass of milk, or something." Her son, a budding Boy Scout, concurred. But I was anxious to keep going in the good weather. They obviously were baffled by my ungrateful behavior.

Soon after that the Trail entered a region of dense timber, beaver ponds, and berry patches. The berries were ripe and bears had been bashing around, trampling the bushes. The raspberries slowed me somewhat but I finally came to Wilson Stream Campsite, where a side trail led to the falls. In the opposite direction another trail led to Jim Whyte's Lookout, said to have been the headquarters of a narcotics smuggling ring in years gone by. While cooking at the campsite I noticed that a fire had burned around the base of a large tree. At Bodfish Intervale the next day they told me that a Ranger on patrol had discovered the smoldering fire and spent most of a day digging it out. Only a complete lack of wind at the time had kept the fire from breaking out.

Bodfish Intervale is a beautiful valley where a settlement once flourished, much like Cades Cove in the Smokies. Only a farm and a few Summer camps were now occupied. The farmer said I could sleep in an abandoned camp across the road, that a storm was coming, and that Jimmy Calloway and Paul Yambert had slept there. They had reported the Trail on Barren-Chairback to be so disrupted by logging that they had gone only ten miles in two days. The drumming of rain on the roof that night made me thankful that I accepted the invitation.

But the rain stopped before daylight and an early start took me around the end of Barren Mountain on a gravel road and up a steep slope to the crest, and a side trail to the lookout on Barren Ledges. The view from this vantage point shows Onawa Lake and Boarstone Mountain beyond. At this point the Appalachian Trail is about six miles from Moosehead Lake at Greenville. The crest of Barren Mountain was a tangle of rocks and roots and gullies, littered with spruce tops. Stumps of white birches jutted up; they had all died years before. Luckily for me someone had more or less cleared the Trail since Jimmy and Paul had come by. The logging had been almost clearcutting. The view from Monument Rock was outstanding, showing numerous lakes and ridges, part of Moosehead Lake, and the Boundary Mountains on the horizon. In the near valley, glamorized by wind clouds and gleaming blue in the bright sunlight, was Long Pond, another of the fine fishing lakes in Western Maine.

On the way down, the Trail was flooded by a beaver pond and wading in kneedeep water was unavoidable. Several acres of trees were dead, drowned by the rising water. At Long Pond the Perhams said they had heard on the radio that I was coming through, and the whole family gathered around to talk. The Perhams were surprised when I didn't stay because it was too early, and suggested staying with "Old John, the Hermit of Pleasant River." He told them he got "goshawful lonesome sometimes." I headed that way along the tote-road but was stopped by darkness and slept in the woods.

The Hermitage was perched on a high bank overlooking Pleasant River, with the road fording the river just below. I was muttering to myself about wading through the icy water when a puzzled exclamation came from the porch of the building, followed by silence, including mine, and then the clatter of a bucket sliding down a cable to the river. Apparently Old John had heard my muttering but didn't see me because of intervening bushes. After staring around he turned a hand winch to draw up the water, then stared around again before going inside. I waded across but was too embarrassed to stop and see Old John.

Upstream from the Hermitage, reached by a side trail, is Gulf Hagas, called by some the "Grand Canyon of the East." Years later, while on a Maine Appalachian Trail Club work trip, I visited Gulf Hagas with Sidney Tappan. Sidney first came to Maine on vacation, met some trail workers, and ended by working harder than if he had stayed at home. The same had happened to Myron Avery, the typical way in which the fever is passed along. The Gulf is a deep and narrow canyon about five miles long, with many waterfalls and pools, and so narrow at some points a person could jump across. During the years when "long logs" were floated down the streams, a giant jam had to be dynamited in the Gulf. One of the men who was lowered on a rope to plant the dynamite was Fred Pittman, Ranger at Katahdin Stream Campsite when I arrived there.

Beyond Pleasant River the A.T. followed the tote-road to White Cap Mountain and followed the telephone line to the Fire Warden's shack. No one was there so I went on to the top, where Bill Danico, of Brownville, was on duty. He was surprised; said people seldom climbed this isolated and rugged peak.

Suddenly, I saw Katahdin, the goal of my walk with Spring, still far away but dominating the scene, jutting from the plateau lake country. Dark areas of spruce around the base and the gray granite above timberline were plainly visible. Actually it is a cluster of peaks, with Baxter Peak as the highest point. Distance by Trail was still about seventy miles, mostly through lake and bog terrain, and Bill didn't believe it could be covered in four days. I told him it's very simple. You just keep walking and walking and walking. Calloway and Yambert had stayed in his shack, and it had taken them an hour to pack their gear. "Looked as though they had bought out an Army and Navy Store," said Bill.

Wading, not hiking, was necessary in a section flooded by a beaver pond on the way down Barren Mountain, between Chairback Mountain and Long Pond.

A sign at a trail junction north of White Cap said the Trail ahead was impassable and to detour via Chadwick Camps. The sign was badly mangled. Mr. Chadwick said it had been done by bears. He also said what I thought were cow tracks were most likely moose, which were increasing since the State had suspended hunting them. Then I came to a lumber camp set up directly on the Trail, and asked a man sitting on a bench which way the Trail went. Instead of answering he said, "Better head for the cook shack over there. Old Johnny Boyle will see that you don't go hungry." He insisted, so I went. Old Johnny was a real character, a rugged individual and a camp cook from the old school. He liked to tell of the days when men were men in the Maine woods, not ordinary six-foot roughnecks. In those days Bill Moranty was King, a mighty man—this tall and this wide—who fought similar giants at every opportunity just for the fun of it. One time Bill went to hunt gold in Alaska. He came back riding a big cowhorse and packing two guns, rode right in the door of the biggest saloon in Big Town, shooting into the ceiling with both hands. They made him County Sheriff and he chased everyone he didn't like clean out of the state.

Meanwhile Johnny placed before me a platter of roast turkey, a big bowl of pea soup, several blueberry pies, and a gallon pot of tea, while apologizing for not having better grub on hand. An hour later Johnny was still talking and I could eat no more, not even blueberry pie. That night I slept—at Johnny's insistence—in the bunkhouse and had breakfast with the crew. I tried to decline a helping of beans, on the excuse that eating almost nothing else for three weeks one time in the South Pacific had left me allergic to them. Johnny heard, and roared, "Ain't no one gets sick from eatin' my beans. You take a plateful." I did and suffered no ill effects. Afterward Johnny told me how to "take the poison out." The logging camp, by the way, was Hillingsworth and Whitney No. 2, operating out of Kokadjo. Nailed to the opposite side of the bunkhouse where the man was sitting the night before was the Trail sign.

The lady at Berry's Yoke Pond Camps had just heard a bulletin on the radio, saw me through the window, and came out to greet me by name. She said she would report my whereabouts as soon as I left, like others had been doing. Her contribution to the Expedition was some pie and milk. Then the Trail swung south around Crawford Pond and north again to Cooper Brook at the falls. Later I spotted moose tracks again, this time with muddy water still in them. Moving slowly around the next bend, camera ready, I heard a sudden crashing in the brush and explosive snorts, obviously a warning signal. Then a grunt came from the bushes in front and a large cow moose, surely one of the homeliest critters on earth, stepped out in the path, stopped, and turned her head in my direction. Snap went the shutter. She turned toward me and stopped again—while I looked for a tree to climb—then she trotted away in the direction of the other moose, probably a yearling calf, with a gait like a bowleg-ged horse, if there is such a thing.

About sunset I came to Antlers Camps, on Lower Jo-Mary Lake, named for a famous Indian guide. The camp owner was away fishing, according to a guest sitting on a cabin porch. She was astonished when I didn't stop, just kept on through the twilight. Except for rainy nights I now preferred sleeping in the open woods, this time along the lake shore. In this area were trees cut by beaver, probably bank dwellers. Next day a man was picking red raspberries and didn't notice my approach. At the sound of my voice he almost jumped over the next bush, probably thinking about bears.

Nahmakanta is one of the largest lakes along the Appalachian Trail. Wind across its wide expanse was kicking up waves that broke on the rocky shore. I cooked dinner at the leanto, then stopped a few miles farther to swim at a sandy beach. Just as I was getting wet a small seaplane, often used in the lake country, zoomed around a headland, sending me scuttling for cover. Some of the bush pilots are legendary, able to land on a beaver pond or a tree-choked stream.

Two hours before sunset I came to Nahmakanta Camps and stopped, intending to visit briefly, then push on to Rainbow Lake Leanto, an easy day's travel from Katahdin. But again it was "Talkin' when I should have been walkin' " and I ended by sleeping in the guide shack. Even so I could have hurried to the end, but the weather was good, had been for a week, and a reluctance to finish the trip was building up. I almost dreaded the time when the Long Cruise would be over. Trail-hiking had become my way of life. Civilization seemed like a sham.

Wind kicked up waves across Nahmakanta, "lake of the largest fish" and, at the time, the largest lake along the A.T.

Early lunch was cooked at Rainbow Lake Leanto, with Katahdin looming high above the tree line on the far shore. Near Rainbow Camps a red fox crossed ahead and then two deer bounded away. In early afternoon the Trail came to the West Branch of the Penobscot River, a turbulent stream linked with many stories and legends of early logging days. It still was serving as a runway for timber, not the "long logs" of early days but the four-foot "sticks" used in pulp making. The cable bridge just above the "Sowdyhunk Falls" had recently been repaired, after damage by ice flood. The falls had been "run" only once, by two Indians in a bateau, with Big Sebattis Mitchell in charge. Another crew, their pride stung, then tried and failed, their bateau crashing and two of them being killed. From the bridge I looked straight down into the maelstrom and wondered how anyone could possibly get through alive.

A fisherman came along and interrupted my reverie. He walked along as far as Little Niagara Falls, where he stopped to fish for trout. The well-worn path then came to Daicey Pond at York's Camps. Katahdin loomed beyond the lake, massive and symmetrical, a beautiful "pile of rocks." That's what Junior York called it. On the lake a man was casting for trout, using either hand, while paddling with the other. Two days later I was to stay at the camp, by invitation of Junior and his mother, before climbing Katahdin a second time with Ward Hinkson and Emlen Cresson, who brought me back to Pennsylvania afterward.

From Daicey Pond the Trail led up to Katahdin Stream Campsite, at the foot of the Hunt Spur. Because of the newspaper and radio ballyhoo I was fearful of what might happen there, but needn't have worried. No one was expecting anyone like me. It would be someone six and a half or seven feet tall, with bright red shirt and hobnailed boots, carrying a high and mighty pack. Actually the real woodsmen of American history, Boone, Crockett, Carson, Wetzel, and others, were of average size and appearance. At any

A cable bridge above "Sowdyhunk Falls" (Nesowadnehunk) spanned the turbulent West Branch of the Penobscot River. The A.T. no longer crosses the river at this point.

rate, the hundreds of campers took no notice of the gray-clad hiker with the low-slung framepack easing along.

The tree line on the far side, beyond the leantos, was close when a stentorian call of "Earl" in Bill Biddle's unmistakable voice told me the jig was up. He came dashing over and said someone had asked if that might be the hiker. Bill was the only one in the campground who had seen me before. He said that Hunt Spur Leanto had burned a few days before so I might as well stay in the campground, at the leanto where he was staying.

According to Bill, the Ranger, Fred Pittman, six feet six and a man of few words, was "really something." Then the Ranger himself approached and asked, "Are you the man walkin' the Trail?" He said he was obliged to phone the lady reporter in Millinocket, that she had threatened to "skin him alive" if he didn't turn me in, no matter what time of day or night. Off he went but soon returned and started talking. Bill just sat, rendered speechless by the Ranger's sudden volubility.

About 11:00 Ranger Pittman came again to announce that Mrs. Dean Chase and Photographer Crowell had arrived and were waiting at Ranger Headquarters. Mrs. Chase interviewed me there and had pictures taken for Associated Press. She promised to wait until I returned from Baxter Peak before releasing the story, provided I promised not to talk with anyone else. A nicer lady could never be found anywhere. Her husband, Dean, was woods boss of the Great Northern Paper Company.

I had to literally crawl out on a limb to photograph the three elements here: "Sowdyhunk Bridge," the falls, and Katahdin, looming in the background.

On the 5th of August, 124 days after leaving Oglethorpe, preparations were made for the Lone Expedition to climb Katahdin. Someone suggested the pack could be left behind but my answer to that was emphatic. That faithful old framepack had come all the way with me from Georgia and it wouldn't be left behind on the last five miles. The weather was good, no cloud cap on the mountain. "Just take it slow and easy," says I to myself, "just like the man in the Smokies said." The Trail ascended through spruce thickets along Katahdin Stream, then crossed a footbridge below the falls and headed for timberline. Near the edge of the trees were fishermen toiling upward, convinced that a fisherman's paradise was somewhere up yonder. Someone must have told them about the Klondike. They stopped at the highest spring. Before me now was the next to the last mile, up the steep and rocky Hunt Spur, where iron rods had been driven into the rocks at some points for hand and footholds.

After an hour of nothing but tip-tilted terrain the Trail suddenly leveled off at the "Gateway," two stones set vertically. Beyond was the tableland, a thousand acres of rock mesa tilted slightly upward to Baxter Peak, about a mile away. In every other direction was spectacular scenery. To the left were other summits of the Katahdin group, the Owl, Barren Mountain, The Brothers, and Doubletop. Below and as far as the eye could reach was a region of lakes, seen as though from an airplane. Among them were Rainbow, Jo-Mary, Nahmakanta, Pemadumcook, and Millinocket, their waters flashing in the noonday sun. Westward were Ripogenus Flowage and Moosehead Lake. Someone has said that a giant mirror was

The next to the last mile for the Lone Expedition was the steep and rocky Hunt Spur, where iron rods had been driven into some rocks for hand and footholds.

The A.T. suddenly leveled off at the "Gateway" to Baxter Peak, only about a mile away. The dual beauty of the "greatest mountain" became evident: it was as glorious to look from Katahdin as to look at it.

broken over Katahdin and the lakes are the pieces. The glory of Katahdin is its dual beauty: to look at, and to look from.

Another mile and the Long Cruise would be over. I almost wished that the Trail really was endless, that no one could ever hike its length. Perhaps in the future it would be extended in a giant loop by way of the Alleghenies, to make it a truly endless trail, more than twice as long. My thoughts were of many places, of memories that would never fade. But time cannot stand still. Like a ship that comes to the quay, its sails furled or its engines quiet, drifting with the impetus of its long voyage, I moved across the tableland. Midway is the solitary Thoreau Spring, discovered on one of the first ascents of Katahdin by Henry David Thoreau, the author of "Walden." Step by step across the rocks the Lone Trail-hiker came to the cairn on Baxter Peak, said to be the first spot in the United States to be touched by the rays of the rising sun. The Little Black Notebook says, "Reached the summit about 1:30."

Beyond was the deep and crater-like bowl of Katahdin, with Chimney Pond Campground directly below. Someone there spotted me against the sky and yodeled a greeting, which I returned. Off to the right were the South Peak and the Knife Edge, most spectacular trail route on Katahdin, its highest point Pamola, goddess of the mountain. I was to hike that narrow crest two days later with Ward Hinkson, Emlen Cresson, and two members of the Mountain Club of Maryland, Bob Stockbridge and Bill Tarbert. Meanwhile, my moccasin boots, like the Wonderful One Hoss Shay, practically disintegrated. But these and others were after-events.

The Long Cruise was finished. Already it seemed like a vivid dream, through sunshine, shadow, and rain—Already I knew that many times I would want to be back again—On the cloud-high hills where the whole world lies below and far away—By the wind-worn cairn where admiring eyes first welcome newborn day—To walk once more where the white clouds sail, far from the city clutter— And drink a toast to the Long High Trail in clear, cold mountain water. Beside me as I stood there, happy yet sad, was another weatherbeaten sign, on a post held up by a heap of gathered stones.

The Lone Trail-hiker posed by the weather-beaten sign which marked the finish of the Long Cruise.